I0884456

Life after Guns

The Rutgers Series in Childhood Studies

The Rutgers Series in Childhood Studies is dedicated to increasing our understanding of children and childhoods throughout the world, reflecting a perspective that highlights cultural dimensions of the human experience. The books in this series are intended for students, scholars, practitioners, and those who formulate policies that affect children's everyday lives and futures.

For a list of all the titles in the series, please see the last page of the book.

Life after Guns

Reciprocity and Respect among Young Men in Liberia

ABBY HARDGROVE

Rutgers University Press
New Brunswick, Camden, and Newark, New Jersey, and London

978-0-8135-7348-9
978-0-8135-7347-2
978-0-8135-7350-2
978-0-8135-7349-6

Cataloging-in-Publication data is available from the Library of Congress.

A British Cataloging-in-Publication record for this book
is available from the British Library.

∞ The paper used in this publication meets the requirements of the American National Standard for Information Sciences—Permanence of Paper for Printed Library Materials, ANSI Z39.48–1992.

www.rutgersuniversitypress.org

Manufactured in the United States of America

For those whose lives fill these pages and for those who read them. We are all students of our human condition and of the worlds in which we live.

Contents

Acronyms

AFL	Armed Forces of Liberia
DDR	disarmament, demobilization, and reintegration
DDRR	Disarmament, Demobilization, Rehabilitation, and Reintegration program
ECOMOG	Economic Community of West African States Monitoring Group
ECOWAS	Economic Community of West African States
LD	Liberian dollars
LURD	Liberians United for Reconciliation and Democracy
MODEL	Movement for Democracy in Liberia
NGO	nongovernmental organization
NPFL	National Patriotic Front of Liberia
PAL	Progressive Alliance of Liberians
ULIMO	United Liberation Movement of Liberia
ULIMO-J	United Liberation Movement of Liberia under Roosevelt Johnson
ULIMO-K	United Liberation Movement of Liberia under Ahlaji Kromah
UN	United Nations

Life after Guns

1
Introduction
Theory, Fieldwork, and Storytelling

I began spending time on Bernard's Beach in Monrovia during 2010, seven years after the final cease-fire that ended fourteen years of civil war in Liberia. The beach was usually quiet. Young men clustered under the coconut trees, out of reach of the sun, talking and smoking and passing the time. There was a pool table and some huddled around the games, taking small bets or waiting to play. Darlington was easy to spot among the others. Always clad in a sleeveless undershirt, shorts, and slippers (flip-flops), he cut a thin male figure, several inches shorter than me. When we met for the first time he informed me that he was security. He kept an eye out for any trouble on the beach as a favor to a friend. Though there were occasional kickbacks for his security work, he made most of his living selling rolled joints on the beach and in the neighboring area. He was a hustler, living on his own in a small room just off the main road. He talked to me at length about studying at a university, but had no money to pay for it. His life and prospects for the future were limited in scope, much like those in ethnographic accounts of other youth in Africa and around the world.

One afternoon while we were passing the time on the beach I asked Darlington to speak about the condition of the country for young men like himself. He sat back, joint in hand, and delivered an articulate analysis of the opportunities available to young people. It included a descriptive account of the implications of poverty, an evaluation of the government's failure to meet the needs of the people—especially the young people—and the reasons beneath local crime and violence. "The helping hand is not there," he finished. So many parents had died or lost the means to support their children, and there was little work. "The helping hand is not there," he reiterated. This book is about the presence and absence of a helping hand in young men's lives, and what that means for their "life chances," a phrase I borrow from Dahrendorf (1981) to indicate the options that people perceive based upon their social positions.

"A helping hand" might refer to a government program or a favor from a friend, but mostly, as Darlington used it, a helping hand meant the support of intergenerational relationships in families and kin networks. Family relations were a constant topic of conversation and concern for the young men in this book. Recent research in youth studies has ballooned with observations and theoretical interpretations about life chances, transitions, and trajectories. An interdisciplinary literature portrays urban young people in the Global South[1] as a marginalized generation (Mains 2012; Resnick and Thurlow 2015; Sommers 2003). More often than not, those who are studied are male. They can be found hustling for subsistence, or sitting with their peers. They are often away from their families, navigating individual trajectories toward uncertain future possibilities. They appear like Darlington and the youth on the beach. For the most part, and with a few exceptions (see Cole and Durham 2007), the intricacies of family life, household reproduction, and intergenerational reciprocity have been largely passed over in the literature. Though their familial networks might have been elsewhere, or fragmented by the destruction caused during the war, reciprocal obligations among family relations were essential to young men's survival and their achievement of social respect in postwar Monrovia, Liberia's capital and largest city. For most, their support networks were too depleted to offer a helping hand for education or livelihood support. The inability to make transitions and sustainable livelihoods is one they share with youth around the world, and which has become so pervasive that it has been described as a "crisis" of youth (International Labour Organization 2013; Richards 1995). However, this book demonstrates that the marginalization felt by young people was not a generational crisis, but rather a crisis felt across generations, and one that had specific implications for young people. It provides an ethnographically grounded analysis of intergenerational hierarchies in Liberia, and illustrates how networks of reciprocal obligation organize social life, forming the foundation of support for young people's lives and future possibilities.

I began this research out of an interest in the life chances of ex-combatants, specifically those who had fought when they were young. Half of the empirical material comes from the postwar experiences of ex-combatant young men. There are two dominant perspectives that inform much of the discourse about "child soldiers": a rights-based narrative that emphasizes how damaging war is for children (see Machel 2001), and a security narrative that constructs former fighters as posing significant risks to postwar stability (see McMullin 2012). I traveled to Monrovia with two related assumptions about young people who live to tell their stories about fighting with armed groups. First, I assumed that they had been deeply affected by their experience, that trauma is a real thing, and that it has lasting impacts on how people live their everyday lives. There is now an enormous amount of research concerned with trauma in the aftermath of war. I conducted this work under the assumption that everyone had been affected by the war, and that while trauma is part of postwar life, it is not the sum total. I have left the analysis of trauma to psychologists and their critics and pursued an ethnographic description of youth experience in the social landscape of the postwar city. Second, in regards to the security narrative, I assumed that ex-combatants *could* pose risks to the well-being of others, but that disruption of the peace was only one among many possibilities on their postwar horizons. In short, this ethnographic account of the experiences of ex-combatant and noncombatant youth in Liberia is designed to offer at least a glimpse of postwar life defined by more than the essentializing "damaged" or "damaging" narratives prolific to the topic of child soldiers and postwar youth. I dedicate much of the narrative work in this book to challenging pejorative assessments of youth as security threats, and argue that such reductionist rhetoric is not merely a limited evaluation of young men, but a deeply destructive force that has its roots in the causes for war itself.

The ex-combatants in this work contribute to an urban understanding of reintegration in Liberia, and their stories provide a glimpse of what fighting and "reintegrating" is like within the city. They are only a few among thousands who have transitioned out of armed groups. It is difficult to account for the volume of lives lived and lost in wars, and especially those who served in armed groups for which we have no enlistment records. The total number of combatants who participated in the war will never be fully known. Approximately 103,000 were disarmed (they turned in one or more weapons), and approximately 101,000 were demobilized (formally discharged from active duty) following the 2003 ceasefire (see McMullin 2013). These numbers account for those who survived the perils of the war and who participated in the United Nations (UN) facilitated disarmament and demobilization process. In the aftermath of wars like this one the UN leads a disarmament, demobilization, and reintegration (DDR) intervention. The goal of this three-pronged approach is to secure weapons, break up factions, and return former combatants to "civilian life." In Liberia, they tacked on a second "R" for rehabilitation. With admittedly minimal resources, the National Commission on Disarmament, Demobilization, Rehabilitation, and Reintegration intended to provide some basic form of group psychosocial counseling and civic engagement along with the vocational skills and training that came under the reintegration program (see UNDP 2003–2004). There are two primary strands of academic literature regarding ex-combatant reintegration, one that informs and critiques demobilization, disarmament, and reintegration policy and practice (see Jennings 2008b; Knight and Özerdem 2004; McMullin 2007, 2012, 2013; Muggah 2009), and the other that looks more intently at the lived experience of social, economic, and political transitions after war (Blattman 2009; Blattman and Annan 2011; Peters 2007; Shepler 2014; Utas 2005a).

The research in this book contributes to both of these strands of inquiry and argument. First, the empirical material is rendered in a comparative perspective. With notable exceptions (see Blattman and Annan 2010), the majority of postwar research about reintegration is conducted with ex-combatants only. Without empirical research with noncombatants, it is difficult to grasp the structure of broader postwar society, or the extent to which ex-combatants face unique challenges in comparison to others—an implicit assumption made by humanitarian discourse, though one that is difficult to challenge or inform without research among young soldiers' noncombatant peers. This ethnographic account demonstrates that social isolation and stigma pose significant challenges to young men, irrespective of whether they fought in the war. However, the implications of stigma and social isolation appear more acutely felt by former fighters who have lost both the helping hand of their previous armed groups, as well as their families. Second, conventional wisdom of the DDR process asserts that armed groups must be demobilized—formally disbanded to prevent further uprising or instability. Though there are cases that confirm this concern,[2] many of the ex-combatants in this research were able to make sustainable transitions to jobs and nonviolent ways of life *specifically because* they were helped and supported by former comrades and commanders, challenging the derogatory notion that networks of former fighters are always and only detrimental social communities. There is also a pragmatic question to be raised around whether "demobilization" is remotely effective. Even within an intentional, lengthy residential program in Liberia, Blattman and Annan (2016) report that combatant networks seemed to retain their strength, even with intensive intervention through psychosocial and vocation training in a designated residential environment. Third, DDR discourse asserts that vocational skills that are appropriate to market needs are essential to sustainable reintegration. There is some evidence to support this. In rural farming contexts, some research finds that ex-combatants who have the appropriate land, resources, training, and monetary incentives have redirected themselves away from illicit activities (Blattman and Annan 2016; Peters 2011). This work demonstrates that in war-torn urban environments like Monrovia there is an enormous amount of human labor, far more than the market can absorb. The ability to "make life," as the young men put it, is far more dependent upon having a helping hand than it is on the acquisition of skills, or entrepreneurial ambition.

Reciprocity and respect are defining themes throughout this work, shaping everyday life, and especially informing ex-combatants' experiences of reintegration. As the book progresses, young people's dignity and the dignity of their fellow Liberians emerges as a central feature of their stories as they are variously positioned within local, national, and international contexts. The dignity of these black men and women on the West African coast has always been in question, since before the nation was founded in the nineteenth century. And in the years following a long and bloody civil war, it remains vital to my account of their lives and their life worlds.

Like Jensen (2008) I did not set out to make dignity a conceptual priority for this research. However, as this book has taken shape I have found myself brought back to questions and observations about dignity as it is claimed, bestowed, or denied in the everyday lives of the people who fill these pages. As dignity surfaces in the following stories, I draw on Jensen's insightful exposition of dignity as a product of dominance. Following Agamben (1999) and Coundouriotis (2006) he understands dignity not as an inherent quality of the self, but as a social distinction bestowed by the state (or the dominant) on certain individuals or groups who are deemed worthy. This inescapable theme is especially present in my understanding of the historical roots of the civil war, and threads throughout my observations of postwar life as it is enabled and inhibited by power relations that extend across local and international contexts.

Structure and Agency

My theoretical orientation to the empirical material is oriented toward inquiry about structure, and how structure shapes and is reinforced by agency, in this case, young men's agency. This theoretical approach elicits an account of social process within context, one that links youth actions to the norms and values of their society, to their relations with the distribution of power or hierarchy in their context, to their lived experiences of exclusion, inequality, or privilege. A structure/agency approach avoids, or at least greatly reduces, the opportunity to misconstrue young men and postwar life based upon my own social and cultural biases—an occurrence all too common in the field of international development. It also, importantly, informs youth experience *with* international humanitarian and security efforts, providing a local description and explanation of young people's "bounded agency" (Evans 2007) from the ground up.

Structure is one of those constructs that, despite prolific use across the social sciences, can prove an elusive concept to pin down (Sewell 1992). Perhaps it should be, as it refers to the "community of dispositions" (Bourdieu 1977) that influences routines and rituals in everyday life, and to the values and norms that guide important social dynamics. These unseen and often unconscious schemas shape society in particular ways, forming distinctions between classes, genders, and generations. Reference to "structure" actually refers to quite a lot, and nothing very specific, unless we set to work observing the social, economic, and political processes that are an outflow of these underpinning values and power relations. In this book, my emphasis is primarily on social structure; I understand political and economic realities as intimately tied to the ways that people relate with, and value one another. "Agency," very simply put, is the ability to act or withhold action (Giddens 1984). As structures inform action in everyday life, they are recursively remade in our social worlds. So, with this research, my aim was to understand how unseen "recipes for action" (Sewell 1992) informed the motions of everyday life, shaping young people's perceived options and possibilities, and how their structural context organized the distribution of resources at macro-levels that encompass politics, economics, and social relations, or in the most basic interactions within households or peer groups.

The analysis I articulate in this book is rendered through a close and descriptive inquiry into everyday life, and the underpinning schemas that inform action. Mains (2012) eloquently describes his work in Ethiopia as a continual movement between the abstraction of articulating broad structural realities and the depth of details explored in the layers and layers of people and places in which he submerged himself on a daily basis. Similarly, in the following chapters I have chosen to spend more time in the personal experiences of everyday life in the postwar capital, though I zoom out at points in order to position actors more proportionately within the broader parameters of their society and their national position in a global context.

"Youth" as Young Men

Young men like Darlington are the subject of this book. Most were between the ages of eighteen and thirty-five. In Liberia, as in most other parts of the world, youth is a social category, defined not so much by age but by one's position in society. Institutions use age ranges to designate who the "youth" are. Many of the UN bodies define youth as between the ages of fifteen and twenty-four. In Liberia, this number was extended to thirty-five (Ministry of Youth and Sports 2005), "to catch everybody in the net," as one youth worker explained. These are merely numerical approximations. Those who are considered youth in Liberia may range in age from thirteen or fourteen well into the midthirties and forties (Moran, 2006). Within the society itself, youth are understood based on their social age, as being in a period between the dependency of childhood and the responsibility and autonomy that comes with adulthood (see Durham 2000). Darlington was in his midtwenties, and had a small child. Though he was a father, he was still considered a youth because he was unable to care for her or support her as a "breadwinning" male. He had yet to become "established." He had no house, no ability to support a wife or a family of his own. He was able to independently support himself through his dealing and was responsible for his own shelter and food. Thus he was no longer dependent on the care of others as he had been in childhood. He could not support dependents of his own, however, a basic social requirement for an adult man.

In this book I focus specifically on young men for reasons that will be discussed later in the section of the introduction to fieldwork. In so doing, my work has fallen into a large body of academic research in which "youth" almost always implicitly refers to young *male* people, whereas studies with young women often have to designate their focus on "female" youth in order to bring attention to otherwise "invisible girls" (Nordstrom 1999). In terms of invoking "youth" as a social construct, most of the young people who are considered youth in Liberia are male. Young women are not expected to experience transitional periods of time between households of caregivers and households of their own. Few undergo a liminal period of caring for themselves and working toward the financial and material status that demonstrates that they are adults, capable of caring for households and families of their own. I found this circumstance only among young women on the street, or those who were engaged in sex work, the two often going hand in hand. Because this in-between period is one of the primary indicators of being a youth, it is often synonymous with being male. Unless otherwise stated, my account of "youth" experience is limited to young men.

Reciprocity and Respect

This research illustrates how young men's life chances, transitions, and trajectories were determined in large part by relationships of reciprocity that enabled and facilitated their achievement of respect. Each of these terms is rendered in specific ways throughout my interpretation of the empirical material. Reciprocity is an essential aspect of Liberians' broader social structure, which is known to anthropologists and Africanists as "wealth in people" (see Guyer and Belinga 1995). Wealth in people organizes a system of people who exchange goods and services for the purpose of maintaining and accumulating social relations that ensure security, labor, and status (see Bledsoe 1980; Newell 2006). The manifestation and function of these relationships is articulated in detail in chapter 3.

Reciprocity itself has long been a point of empirical inquiry and theoretical debate among anthropologists. Lemarchand (1989) observes that the literature tends to fall along something of a continuum, with interpretations of exchange as a moral imperative on the one end, and as a strategic and functional social practice that ensures production on the other. In this work I understand reciprocity as a pragmatic necessity undergirded by moral values. Fulfilling obligations to reciprocate earns the respect of one's social community and the recognition that one has conformed to the social structure that organizes everyday life.

Respect is intrinsically about one's social standing and status in a given context. Respect, respectability, and dignity have featured in recent work with young people, especially marginalized young men (Di Nunzio 2012; Jensen 2008; Newell 2012), as their struggle for value and recognition in society is frustrated by economic, political, and social constraints. Dignity becomes an issue or a struggle when dominance produces humiliation (Jensen 2008) or "abjection," that sense of being thrown down or excluded by boundaries that confine agency, and are largely determined by the "dominant cultural fraction" (Mahar 1990). Bourgois's (2003) evocative and seminal work among crack dealers in Harlem illustrates how political and economic systems were set up in such a way as to deny access to sustainable economic opportunities, producing exclusion for his informants, most of whom became involved in drug dealing. The structure of a society, the values that underpin social worth, the distribution of political power and economic opportunities, creates access for some and inhibits access for others. Dignity and abjection are inherently structural. The social values that imbue or deny dignity are produced and reproduced by agency. As long as actors assimilate and accommodate the terms by which dominance bestows dignity, then those terms, and the struggle to achieve dignity, will persist.

Jensen's (2008) iteration of the struggle for dignity in South Africa closely resembles the search for respect among Bourgois's (2003) informants in Harlem. In this work I draw a conceptual distinction between the two terms. Dignity has to do with values that bestow worth. The struggle for dignity is the struggle for worthiness. When I speak about respect I am referring to something related to, but distinguished from, dignity. Respect manifests in two forms, for which I borrow Spencer's (1965) constructs of "honor" and "prestige." Honor is associated with socially acceptable conduct or benchmarks of achievement, and prestige is obtained through success in competition with peers.

On first glance honor and dignity may appear conflated but they are not. In the following chapter we will see how the dominant cultural fraction of elite Americo-Liberians set the terms for inclusion in political power and access to resources. They confined access to their group. Though indigenous Liberians sought socioeconomic mobility in the urban capital and came to value emblems of modern and American culture—hallmarks of elite society—they were fundamentally denied equal opportunities to achieve the structural positions enjoyed by the dominant. They could be honorably providing for families through socially acceptable means and conduct, yet as long as their pursuit of social worth conformed to the terms of the minority elite dignity would always remain largely out of their grasp. Thus it was possible to achieve honor and prestige in the sight of one's peers and community, while struggling to obtain dignity determined by the regard of the dominant cultural fraction. In summary, dignity is about worth. Honor is about conduct. And prestige is about achievement in competition or comparison with peers.

A sense of abjection and struggle for dignity mounted, creating the conditions that led to the inception of war. Before embarking on that analysis I would like to turn our attention to the young people who transitioned into armed groups, who fought in their ranks, and to how I have conceptually understood their "reintegration."

Ex-Combatants and Reintegration

Who are the ex-combatants, and what does "reintegration" actually mean? Some scholars use a wide conceptual definition for "ex-combatants" in regards to the roles that they fill with armed groups. Some include, in addition to the armed fighters, the men, women, and children who acted in noncombat support roles like cooks and porters (see Gates and Reich 2009; Guyot 2007). In contrast, Lemasle (2010) limits her use of "ex-combatants" to those who have actively fought and are in positions to use arms to disrupt postwar peace. Such variations in definition may be relevant to these and other contexts. During fieldwork I spoke with people who had been forced to fulfill service roles that included cooking and carrying possessions, equipment, and supplies as porters. However, they did not identify as ex-combatants, nor were they identified as such by others. Similarly, though Darlington and I never discussed this, a friend of his alluded to his participation with one of Charles Taylor's militias. Darlington carried a gun for a short while, and held some form of security and combat support responsibilities during the later years of the war. However, he never identified, and was never identified by his peers, as an "ex-combatant." Thus, the only people I have chosen to refer to as "ex-combatants" are those who self-identified with that term and were identified in their community as former fighters. It should also be noted that I use "combatant," "fighter," and "soldier" interchangeably. I am certain that there are instances in which these terms require distinction. For this work, I see no need to do so, and have chosen to alternate the use of them to provide some variation in vocabulary. Some young men fought during most of the fourteen years of civil crisis. Others served shorter periods. The common denominator is their participation and affiliation with a fighting force that separates their wartime experience from those of noncombatants. All of them were young when they were incorporated into their units. Most were in their teens or early twenties, and by any definition were considered "youth" at the time of their conflict participation.

The label "ex-combatant" is layered with meanings. Former fighters and others appropriate it in order to meet certain ends (McMullin 2012), and there is undoubtedly some error or misappropriation in much of its use, no matter the specificity applied. For example, a huge signifier of ex-combatant identity was attached to those who participated in the UN-led Disarmament, Demobilization, Rehabilitation, and Reintegration (DDRR) program. It publicly identified participants as former combatants in the civil war. Participants were given ID cards to identify them as ex-combatants who were enrolled in the program.[3] However, given the amount of money offered in the Transitional Safety Net Allowance (see UNDP 2003–2004), it is unquestionable that some of the participants presented guns and signed up for the program to claim the 300 U.S. dollars in cash even though they were never actively involved in the combat or with armed groups. Jake, who features later in this chapter and others, was never a fighter, nor did he belong to an armed group. However, when they were offered the opportunity to participate in DDRR, his friends in a rebel group gave him a gun to turn in so that he could claim the cash assistance. At the same time, many women did not participate in DDRR. Among the most pronounced reasons for this was a heightened fear of gendered stigma and exclusion in the postwar environment (see Christoffersen 2010; Coulter, Persson, and Utas 2008). They were afraid that as women they would be treated with more severe disregard than their male counterparts. Thus, there is some margin for error no matter the discursive or institutional parameters in place. Suffice it to say, everyone included in this research identified themselves as ex-combatants.

We have arrived at ex-combatant "reintegration," a construct often synonymous with the implementation of policies and programs, though as a term it suggests an experienced process, or a transition of some kind. "Integration" means being incorporated, or not differentiated from others. Reintegration as a UN policy and program is a security measure designed to help ex-combatants to adjust to "normal life" through economic and social supports (UN 2016). It is framed as an attempt to put ex-combatants "back" (McMullin 2013). That there is a "normal life" to be put back into is an enormous assumption that compels an array of questions. Back where? Back with whom? Back into what exactly? What is "normal"? The policy narrative implicitly frames "civilian life" as normal, and conflict or life in armed groups as abnormal. I do not wish to digress into a lengthy deconstruction of such an obtuse term as "normal." Rather, I would like to point out how dichotomous and unidirectional this notion is. In the UN and other international policy discourse, "reintegration" of ex-fighters implies an assumption that the physical and social structures of communities exist in static form (Boersch-Supan 2009). It assumes that society is a homogenous "field," unitary, whole, and *different* from the wartime life experienced by fighters. The narrative implicitly draws a rigid line between the kind of people who fight war and the kind of people who do not, and assumes that one must become like the other. Thus "reintegration" is represented as a kind of "going back to," as though these structures have been unchanged and are ready and able to receive and resituate former soldiers who "return" to civilian society (Schafer 2007). In fact, wars may deeply change communities. Combatants do not reintegrate into what was, but must integrate along with the rest of the nation into what is becoming. It is a process of "motion within motion" (Vigh 2009).

Having problematized the term, I have chosen to keep and use it in this book, though I understand it more broadly and with fewer dichotomous connotations. In this work reintegration is first and foremost a social process, though it certainly intersects with and has implications for economics and politics. As the following section and chapter 6 will make clear, ex-combatants do have to negotiate transitions from lives shaped and enabled through social structures in armed groups to lives defined and empowered differently in other social arenas after war. Former fighters make decisions about which social norms and values to reject, retain, or reconfigure after conflict, and those decisions carry significant implications for incorporation in communities of noncombatants. So too, noncombatants exercise their agency, their acceptance, their rejection, or ambivalence regarding ex-combatants in their lives and their communities. This means that reintegration is a transactional process that occurs over time among and between former fighters and noncombatants. This being the case I have made a discursive choice not to use the term "civilian," as once they are disarmed and demobilized, ex-combatants are civilians as well, and the postwar space is one that belongs to them, and is shaped through their agency as much as through anyone else's.

About Guns

The depiction of wars that incorporate young people have become synonymous with images of AK-47s, the assault rifles designed in the Soviet Union at the end of World War II, and that continue to be brandished by young children, youth, and adults in conflicts around the globe. War is much more than guns, or the violence dealt at the tip of a gun barrel. It is not my intention to reproduce a stereotype with the title "Life after Guns." However, in the Liberian context of my research, guns were a defining feature of the conflict for those who participated and for those who were affected directly and indirectly by a war waged in their backyards, on their streets, and in the bush. Guns symbolized what Shaw (2000) refers to as a "habitus of war," in which violence became an integral part of the environment. Social and cultural reproduction continued, adapted, and reconfigured with the perpetuation of violence and armed conflict. Life did not stop because of the war, but it was drastically altered as a result of it. For the fighters, guns were a source of immense power, unlike anything they had experienced before.

"When I was a soldier I could go anywhere," Jacob explained. A twenty-eight-year-old ex-combatant, he related well the sense of agency that many remembered fondly from their time with armed groups. "Anything I wanted I could get it. I got money. Anytime, anything I wanted, I get it. I bust people's door, I bust people's store. I take it. That's when I had the arm [gun]."

The gun was a symbol of power for ex-combatants—power to combat foes, power to direct subordinates, and power to control unarmed civilians. Guns were the instruments that enabled otherwise small, relatively uneducated, and unskilled young people to take lives, to force old and young to fetch and carry, to go or stay. The "gun sound" instilled fear, sent people running into hiding in their homes, into the bush, and across borders. Memories of the beginning and the end of the war were invoked most often by reference to the sound of guns.

In the small community of Slipway, an elderly woman sat and talked with me one day, and related simply, "But for me, I alright now. There's no gun sound. You can walk in peace."

Life after Guns is an exploration of what it meant for young people to be armed, unarmed, and disarmed in the years during and after the Liberian civil war. It is about the social practice that enabled survival and imbued status among those who fought as well as those who did not.

Fieldwork

I spent seven months in the field during 2010 and 2011 conducting ethnographic research in the greater Monrovia area. I rented a room in Central Matadi, a community located just behind Sinkor, to the east of downtown. Most of the homes were made of cement block and painted in bright colors, a structural and aesthetic step up from the straw woven huts or zinc sheets that sheltered those with the fewest means. Schools were dotted throughout the community, and the roadsides were peppered with small stands where young men sold phone credit, charged cell phones, and changed money. Much of my analysis is the result of living alongside the families whose houses framed the parameter of my backyard. Though I was considered a guest throughout my stay, and never fully integrated into the routines of household reproduction, being grafted into the goings-on with the family and our social life in the yard was invaluable to my understanding of daily life and social process.

I gained access to a number of communities around the city, where I spent time with unoccupied youth, conducted informal and semistructured interviews, and implemented focus groups. I always entered with an introduction of some kind—through a pastor, a youth worker, or a friend. The ex-combatants and street youth were the most suspicious, and building trust was not as quick or as easy as with others. That is quite understandable. Monrovia was a bastion for international journalists and researchers after the war. Many Liberians felt raked over by impersonal and exploitative interest in their postwar plight. One afternoon my research assistant took me out to meet some young people in Red Light, the largest market within the capital city region. They were loud and rowdy, and some were agitated when Zawoo explained my purpose for being there. One responded, "All these people come in here. They get the stories and they leave and make money from them. We can't see *nah-ting*!"

I heard the same thing in Bernard's Farm, and Slipway, and from people who were formally a part of the research as well as others who were not. Assurances that my work was not a pathway to becoming rich and famous on my return to the university did little to ease the minds of the skeptical, most of whom had felt used and looked at, without being cared for or seen. With most, I built rapport slowly, over hours spent watching the pool on Bernard's Beach, smoking cigarettes with young men in Red Light and Slipway, and through respectful introductions made by allies to the work. On a visit to Gardnersville, an ex-combatant described his reluctance about my work: "This man [Jake] came to me and convince me. He came to me first, he told me [about you]. I say 'I refuse.' I say, 'I don't want for anybody to interview and take any statement from me.' But he still try to convince me this morning. And he went for me at the house. That how I came."

"What did he say to convince you?" I asked.

"Really, he's my brother, because he and I live together before. We did things in common. He said, 'the woman means nothing. She only came to do a study with me. She came to find . . . she came on a'—how you call it?"

"On a research," Jake interjected affirmatively.

"Research! 'Yeah, she don't mean no harm. She only want to talk to you, to get your view . . .' That's what he told me. So I said, 'I ain't got problem with that, so I will go.'"

Initial introductions like the ones Jake made in Gardnersville began the "snowball." Once established in these communities, my informants could identify others who were willing to contribute to the work.

I used various qualitative methods in six areas around the city. I spoke with ex-combatants in Bernard's Farm, Gardnersville, and Slipway in an attempt to find common themes about reintegration that were not particular to one community or subgroup. Most hailed from Charles Taylor's forces, though I did not specifically target his recruits. As Taylor was based in Monrovia from 1996 to 2003, when the war ended, it makes sense that there would be many of his former troops settled within the region. Young men on Bernard's Beach and in the park at the University of Liberia informed my understanding of postwar life chances and trajectories for noncombatant youth. In Red Light, my participant observation and interviews with youth on the street illustrated the constraints of life lived without intergenerational networks of support. This is a reality that many ex-combatants faced once their factions were disbanded. I wanted to comprehend the challenge of everyday life for the street youth in order to better grasp any added or different challenges that compounded the everyday struggle to "make life" among ex-combatants who finished the war but did not "have people" who would be part of that process with them.

The majority of young people who fought in the war were male, and I chose to limit my work to male experience. I have not offered a significantly gendered analysis because I do not have the comparative female data that would allow me to specify what aspects of life chances or trajectories are gendered in certain ways. With a larger research budget and more time, this would have been a priority. As it is, I chose to use my time and resources to focus on a comparison of young men who fought and young men who did not.

Finally, I looked to elders who could inform my interest in intergenerational relations, and who could offer perspectives that would inform, compare, and contrast the perspectives that youth provided. Zawoo, who was an invaluable support and contributed a wealth of insight to this project, led several focus groups with me in West Point and in Slipway. These added to numerous interviews I had with adults in other communities and with an important contingent of youth workers who had been on the frontlines of the reintegration and rehabilitation programs that were rolled out in the months and years following the 2003 cease-fire. Confidentiality was of utmost importance to many of the people who offered their stories and their thoughts to this work. Pseudonyms have been assigned to all informants in order to protect their privacy.

Telling Other People's Stories

Weber ([1904] 2004, 374) reminds us that "there is no 'objective' analysis of 'social phenomena' *independent* of special and 'one-sided' perspectives, on the basis of which such phenomena can be (explicitly or implicitly, consciously or unconsciously) selected as an object of research, analysed and systematically represented." As an ethnographer, I was the instrument of research. The materials collected for this work were my field notes, jotted from my observations, and transcripts and notes taken down from my conversations. They have been pulled together to present aspects of other people's lives, and to demonstrate what I see as important for our understanding of their life chances in a postwar environment. As such, I have thought much about my own involvement in the research and how I present those who participated.

Bourgois (2003, 2009) worries about the problems that come with examinations of social marginalization and the politics of representing the experiences of the poor. He fears that viewing and appropriating meaning to another's life and life circumstances could easily slip into preconceived stereotypes, and the research itself could be perceived as an exercise in voyeurism. I would argue that this is a risk in research with any demographic, though perhaps it tends to render the ethnographer more self-conscious in research with the poor, as we perceive them in positions with less of a platform to give voice to the constraints in which they live. That is an uncomfortable dynamic to sit with, and one that many scholars wrestle with as they traverse boundaries of all kinds. Throughout this work I have felt acutely the words of Jamaican posse member Brambles to Laurie Gunst during her work in the underworld of Kingston ghettos (Gunst 1996, 127–128):

> To enter into the study of this ghetto society requires a certain kind of courage. . . . It is an enormously variegated and complex subject. Those willing to take on the task must have an active, energetic mind capable of putting together infinite numbers of observations and events into something approaching a meaningful whole. . . . To think and work in such a manner requires intellectual openness. Agility. Or the person must face the distinct prospect of being overwhelmed by the breadth and depth of social and political phenomena. . . . I have seen the incipience of intellectual arrogance in you, and sometimes you question the credibility of events. You are entering a new experience. You are writing something unique. You are white. It is difficult for a white person to simulate a black experience. And it is even more difficult to express or interpret something you have never experienced. Be calm.

I rarely felt "agile" in my movements through Monrovia, with the youth in the market and on the beach, or even in my backyard. And I have been overwhelmed by the immensity of this task—small as it is—from the moment I began it. Nonetheless, I feel compelled by the work of authors like Bourgois and Gunst who, despite entering contexts that were not their own, were able to reflect back to a broader audience the destruction of violence spread unequally through the world, and the ways and means by which it maintains exploitative power. I was young, and white, and "other" in the context of my fieldwork, and my position in an unequal world absolutely shaped the course of the research, the access I gained, and the story I have told. I say all of this not to issue a caveat about the integrity of the empirics, but to acknowledge where they are subject to my own subjectivities and to those who shared their lives with me. As Lammers (2006) writes of her work with ex-combatants and displaced youth in Kampala, Uganda, the work itself occurs between the lives of real people interacting with a living anthropologist, and the authenticity of the work is bolstered by our attentiveness to the variegated complexities that Brambles so eloquently describes.

Brambles was right. It is difficult to express or interpret something I have not experienced. At best, this is an ethnographic sketch of young men's life chances in a postwar terrain. Much like Zeitlyn's (2008) description of a silhouette, my aim is a proportionate outline of actors in context, being honest about the incompleteness of the representation, and striving for faithfulness around the edges—without romanticizing the resilience of those subject to degradation, or gawking at displays of violence in an "exotic" context. I have sought to render their stories with as much intellectual openness as I am able, and to articulate the struggles they face with an analytical scope set wide enough to see the structures that constrain and inhibit, as well as the possibilities that remain.

2

A History of Violence

Young people, especially young men, are regularly subjected to what I refer to in this book as the "loose molecules paradigm." Kaplan (1996) famously (perhaps infamously) described West African youth as loose molecules in an unstable social fluid. His evocative assessment depicts young people as detached, unstable, and potentially explosive, objectifying a generation of young men as a hazardous material exposed in a combustible environment. Though his discursive representation of young men might be discounted as the sensational amplifications of a journalist, such notions about youth have gained traction in academia and policy discourse. Singer (2010, 97) argues that "once the ratio of young males grows too far out of balance, violent conflict tends to ensue." They are by nature more psychologically aggressive, he continues. They are thus biologically predisposed to violence, and a deadly force to be reckoned with should their numbers grow out of proportion. The panic over young men increases when the "Youth Bulge Hypothesis" is thrown into the mix, as it identifies countries with high percentages of youth as especially prone to armed conflict and civil war (Urdal 2004, 2006). Though this is an observed correlation—and not a direct cause—it is easily extrapolated by observers as further fuel to the loose molecules paradigm. Writing for the World Bank, Lin (2012) discusses youth in developing countries as a "demographic dividend or a demographic bomb," reproducing a notion of youth as a highly explosive and destructive force. This ideology has gained traction in policy discourse, where the assumption has taken hold that unemployment and "idleness" lead to conflict (see Walker et al. 2009, 29–38), despite evidence to the contrary (Bøås and Hatløy 2008). The implication of young men as sources of instability fuels the "threat narrative" (McMullin 2012) in postwar policy, reducing ex-combatants to security risks that must be managed and contained to preserve peace.

This essentializing discourse is associated with the "New Barbarism" (Richards 1996), a racist orientation toward Africa and African conflicts that "assumes that conflict makes no sense according to outsiders' rules and must be a throwback to some African 'Dark Age'" (ibid., xxi; see also McMullin 2012). In short, young people and the wars they fight are the results of some sort of primal, inherently violent nature that plagues the continent and thwarts sustainable peace and development. The New Barbarism places blame on (presumably) violent youth and their presumably amoral, "belligerent" (see Achvarina and Reich 2006), venal leaders like Charles Taylor, neglecting the role of regional and international structures and power dynamics (McMullin 2012). This chapter provides a historical overview that stands in stark contrast to such reductionist views of the African continent and the country of Liberia. My aim is to challenge the fixation with violent young black men by repositioning our focus on the long history of structural violence that led to the war in which they fought and from which everyone struggled to recover. I trace the roots of the Liberian civil war to the abjection and exploitation of a whole group of people in the United States, an abjection that was transplanted to the West African coast, where it took root in the founding of the nation. Richards (2006) reminds us that wars do not merely "erupt." They are, among other things, social projects. The social foundation for the civil war in Liberia was laid through over a hundred years of structural violence, in which ideas about social identities shaped political and economic forces that created unequal access to rights, privileges, and services.[1] In short, the war was caused by the assertion of dominance, the denial of dignity, and a long-fought and multifaceted struggle to reclaim it.

The Colonial Movement for Freed Slaves

In their Declaration of Independence from Great Britain, the American authors penned a challenge to structures that confer abjection. They asserted that all men were created equal, with certain unalienable rights—the right to life, liberty, and the pursuit of happiness. Shortly after the American Revolution several socioeconomic and politically charged issues surfaced with regard to the issue of slavery. Freed from the oppression of colonial rule, this newly independent country was instituted by a dominant group of white immigrants who lived and made livelihoods and profits from the labor of enslaved black men, women, and children. Samuel Johnson captures well the irony of the slave trade in colonial America with his question, "How is it that we hear the loudest yelps for Liberty among the drivers of negroes?" (quoted in Shick 1977, 2).

The architects of governance in the United States were not blind to the moral inconsistency in their society. Contestation abounded over what solutions could be applied to the problem of slavery in America. The subjugation of so many black slaves[2] over so many generations created a multitude of challenges that would not be met solely through the act of emancipation. A number of key figures in the early years of nation building, among them Thomas Jefferson, James Madison, and James Monroe, began advocating for emancipation, followed by the relocation of freed slaves outside the United States (Shick 1977). To remove the subjected population of black slaves appeared a far more durable and efficient solution than to address the gross inequalities that separated slaves from freed men, and to integrate as equals those who had been cast down for so long. In a letter to John Lynd, Thomas Jefferson (1811) wrote that it was "most desirable," that emancipation to another land would be advantageous "for gradually drawing off this part of our population." He continued, "Most advantageous for themselves as well as for us; going from a country possessing all the useful arts, they might be the means of transplanting them among the inhabitants of Africa; and would thus carry back to the country of their origin the seeds of civilization, which might render their sojournment here a blessing, in the end, to that country."

The American Colonization Society was founded in 1816. It adopted a public rhetoric for a movement that echoed Jefferson's sentiments. The project presented a "win-win" situation that would, in theory, benefit everyone. A colony of freed slaves in Africa would rid white Americans of the social and moral problem of slavery by "drawing off" the unwanted people among them. Evangelical Christian preaching ascribed great spiritual significance to the project of sending freed slaves who were somewhat "civilized" back to Africa. They believed that an African colony would be a "promised land" for freed slaves, much like the land of Israel in the Bible (Shick 1977).

By colonization, Jefferson and others meant *only* a colony in the sense of a settlement. The intended U.S.initiated settlement in West Africa did not at the outset have the political or economic ambitions that European colonialism did. Expulsion, rather than territorial exploitation, was the primary goal. Exploitation was forthcoming in the years following the establishment of Liberia. However, at its inception the project was one of population removal, and not an investment in an American political appendage abroad (Liebenow 1962).

In 1820, efforts to establish the first settlement of freed American slaves came to fruition. On April third the *Elizabeth* set sail for the African coast with eighty-eight free blacks on board (U.S. State Department 2015). Most were former slaves on Southern plantations, and few had received any formal education. These first sojourners would be the forefathers and mothers of the nation of Liberia. Subsequent voyages transplanted additional freed men and women, though such efforts were hardly enough to quell the coming storm of civil war in the United States—a war fought chiefly over the right to own slaves. Though the project had gained significant momentum and support, there were those who saw no benevolence in the endeavor. In staunch opposition to the movement, antislavery activist Giles Stebbins (1853) later wrote of the American Colonization Society, "Its highest form of philanthropy toward the coloured man is to send him to Liberia. As for treating him as a man here, that is a different matter—the obligation to do so it repudiates—for slavery has created a stern and cruel prejudice, forbidding such treatment, and the easiest way to keep up this prejudice is to talk about African civilization."

Those who left the United States for Africa met with unsurprisingly difficult odds. After a failed attempt to establish a settlement in Sierra Leone, President James Monroe sent U.S. naval officer Lieutenant Robert Field Stockton to the colonists with instructions to use whatever means necessary to procure land for a viable settlement. Stockton and his associate, Dr. Eli Ayers, cruised the coastal area until they came upon what appeared to be a suitable location in Cape Mesurado, in what is now modern-day Liberia. Upon arrival in 1822, Lieutenant Stockton and Dr. Ayres engaged in several fruitless land negotiations with a native chief, King Peter, who eventually declined to engage in further meetings with them. Undeterred, the Americans plunged into the bush and made their way to his village. When their insistence failed to result in a land deal and the atmosphere became noticeably tense, Stockton and Ayers drew pistols on the chief. Given the display of force, King Peter conceded to the Americans' wishes. He sold them a selected area of land for a payment made in guns, beads, tobacco, gunpowder, rum, and various other goods. Numerous subsequent conflicts ensued between the indigenous tribes and the newly arrived colonists from America.[3]

The early settlers arrived on the continent under the auspices of a "civilizing" mission. They have been understood as elitist, even "pompous" (Shick 1977). Western style dress, attendance at church and other social activities, and proper spoken English were hallmarks of their early communities. I spoke with a government official who referred to his forefathers as having "that top-hat mentality." The "cultural style" (Ferguson 1999) that set them apart from their neighbors has been interpreted as a sign of an arrogant and naïve population group. Such assessments may reflect historical realities, though it seems fair to keep in mind that the culture from whence they came was also the only one they knew. It seems reasonable, for example, that they would reproduce American dress. By any account, the settlers' way of life struck a sharp contrast between themselves and the indigenous communities around them. As their settlements expanded and developed it became evident that they wished to maintain a separation that was as economic and political as it was social and cultural.

Internal Mismanagement and International Dependence

National sovereignty was officially established in 1847. The constitution and model of government were fashioned after that of the United States. From the founding of the Republic, Liberia was plagued by a series of economic crises that were alleviated through increased dependence on external actors, mainly in the United States. The early settler economy proved dysfunctional. During the initial settlement, immigrants were given land to cultivate (10–25 acres). However, the understandable distaste for agricultural work among recently liberated slaves, and the unsuitable tools provided by the American Colonization Society led most settlers to engage in two forms of economic activity: trade and politics. Trade was a challenge, as the indigenous tribes had a long-established relationship with European traders. The Americo-Liberians, as they became known, could not compete with indigenous communities who met traders all along the coast. The Ports of Entry Law addressed this dilemma in 1864. It limited the number of ports accessible to foreigners so that taxes could be enforced. This also inhibited indigenous tribes from trading with the Europeans. Further uprisings ensued as a result. Internally, corruption and embezzlement thwarted the economic capacity of the government (van der Kraaij 1983). By the turn of the century, the new nation was faced with a depleted budget and little manpower to oversee expanded government administration in the interior. The government was so destitute that it had already been forced to take out two loans, one in 1871 and another in 1906. Additional loans were taken out in 1912 and 1917.

It was against this backdrop of severe economic insufficiency and dependence that the infamous Firestone agreements came about.[4] American businessman Harvey Firestone was in the market for rubber in the late 1920s and early '30s. He found it in Liberia. His company leased one million acres for a period of ninety-nine years at a rate of six cents per acre per annum. At that time, the government of Liberia required a sum of five million dollars to run the country. Firestone offered a loan, but the government refused. They insisted that too much power would be granted to one hand. Firestone then created the Finance Corporation of America with the help of some U.S. congressmen. The government of Liberia subsequently received pressure from the U.S. State Department and considerable encouragement from their *own* President Charles King and former president Arthur Barclay and Senator William Tubman—both having been hired to serve as Firestone's company lawyers in Liberia (van der Kraaij 1983).

The government of Liberia agreed to a loan taken out with the Finance Corporation of America, a decision that was perhaps more serious than the exorbitant amount of land they had leased to Firestone. With this agreement, Liberia became a country "virtually under control of American administrators appointed by a Government on the other side of the Atlantic" (van der Kraaij 1983, 49–50). With the Firestone Concession and the loan agreement, Liberia conceded a significant amount of economic and political control to an *international corporation* backed by the U.S. government.

Given the financial constraints, expansion of governance outside of Monrovia was relatively infeasible. The indigenous tribes were incorporated beneath the governance of the elite central government in Monrovia *without* equal representation within that body. Indigenous leaders agreed to the terms on the understanding that they would have better leverage with the American government. The result was not at all what they had hoped for. Chiefs could be sent to present problems to the legislature. They were required to pay a $100 delegate fee for the privilege to present their case. However, they were given no voting rights in the legislature. Renegotiations on the matter were futile. Tribal authorities were offered some degree of jurisdiction over matters of justice and commerce in the interior. They saw this as a useful way to improve links to the central government in Monrovia while maintaining certain degrees of authority in their own regions (d'Azevedo 1969). By the 1930s, during President King's term of office, the transition to incorporation was acutely felt. One Gola elder explained (d'Azevedo 1969, 55): "We old men were treated no better than small boys in the time of King. He overlooked us, and untrained young men and strangers were made into chiefs over us. Commissioners could place us in stocks before our own people and bad men from Monrovia could take our wealth with the help of such chiefs. We were helpless and our people wept." The exploitation and manipulation d'Azevedo captures in this elder's sentiments reflect a common theme in Liberian history. Over the course of more than a century practices of exclusion and differential incorporation solidified the social, economic, and political divide between urban Americo-Liberians and the rural majority.

Growth without Development, Integration without Inclusion

William V. S. Tubman was elected in 1944 and remained president until he died in 1971. Great value was placed on "civilized" and modern education during the Tubman years. As a nation, Liberia experienced perhaps the most significant transformations during his long tenure. There were two policies that defined his presidency—the Unification Policy and the Open Door Policy. With them, Liberia experienced tremendous growth and structural integration between the urban elite and indigenous majority, though by the time of Tubman's death in 1971 it was apparent that the nation had achieved neither true unification nor lasting development.

Under the Unification Policy, Tubman sought to formally integrate the indigenous majority, ending a long tradition of indirect rule. He extended suffrage to all property owners and to those who paid their hut tax (Rinehart 1985). With the Unification Policy Western educational institutions began to take precedence over the traditional rural education in secret societies (the nature of which will discussed more fully in chapter 5). This educational transition was facilitated in part through the accommodation of Western Christian missionaries and educators in the interior. What was modern, urban, and Western took precedence over rural cultural and social practices.

The sociopolitical division between the elite minority and everyone else was further established with the economic developments that came in conjunction with these political developments. By the end of the Second World War, a port had been built in Monrovia, an international airport had been completed, and notably, the Firestone Rubber plantations had been established after the company was granted a ninety-nine year concession to a million acres in 1926. These were the first large-scale employment opportunities that incorporated indigenous Liberians into the wage economy. Wrubel (1971, 193) concludes, "Given access to a great many elements of western culture (a hallmark of the settler group), the large numbers of tribal people who had left their traditional villages would clearly become increasingly conscious during the 1950s of the evidences of differential incorporation." In fact, the inequality was so apparent that Fraenkel (1964, 225) captures a prediction of civil war from a young university student who stated bitterly of the Americo elite, "these people are too hard in their hearts, they cannot change . . . There will be a civil war. They think so much of themselves, and who are they?" Although President Tubman spoke frequently on the importance of unification and equality, these statements were more symbolic than substantive. During Tubman's long tenure, public services expanded, revenue increased, and the number of resources for distribution grew. None of these advances, however, were significant in equalizing the two major social groups. Privileges and opportunities—social, economic, and political—continued to be accessible only to the dominant minority (Wrubel 1971).

In the 1940s, education became a primary source of socioeconomic mobility. Moving to Monrovia for educational attainment became a growing trend among the indigenous people.

The population of Monrovia doubled between 1963 and 1972.[5] The educated people who had integrated (as much as possible) into Americo society strongly believed in unification. Those who were loyal to Americo society received low-level political leadership (Hlophe 1979). A new social class of technocrats emerged. These were educated indigenous Liberians who had established themselves in midlevel management positions in the urban sector. Nonetheless, family affiliations with the Americo elites remained important social and economic links. What the indigenous people could not seem to obtain were upper-level political positions. These remained firmly in the grasp of the elite families in the ruling class (Hlophe 1979).[6]

In 1952 Tubman's Open Door Policy continued a pattern of growth without development (Osaghae 1996). With this policy Liberia opened to foreign business of a particular kind. The policy allowed foreign businesses to invest. However, the constitution of Liberia forbade citizenship to white people. The Tubman administration refused to provide investment incentives to black investors from neighboring countries while granting them to foreign white investors who could not be citizens, vote, or run for public office. This ensured that foreign stakeholders would not be able to become citizens and thereby involve themselves in internal politics. This strategy had two further implications. As in the case of Firestone, it further tied the economic growth of the country to the interests of foreigners, rather than to Liberians. It also thwarted the entrepreneurial efforts of a rising middle class of indigenous Liberians. Foreign investors could come in with business plans and access to capital that few of the middle class could rival.

In short, the policy isolated economic opportunities from the indigenous community as well as from surrounding African nations. The Americo-Liberian elites were able to maintain dominance by relying on the work and investment of foreigners to generate economic growth. The majority of companies and corporations involved in lucrative enterprises like mining and rubber were either solely or jointly owned by foreign businesses or the government of Liberia, or both (van der Kraaij 1983). Thus the country was run by an elite minority that offered the resources of a rich land to international investors. This political and economic development "from without" led Horton (1994, 2) to reflect, "The buildings, bridges, communication and transportation facilities, rubber and mining operations, and everything else that indicated development to me were not true development. They were mere installations, not representative of the Liberian people's creativity and inventiveness. They could not be sustained without white foreigners and were certain to crumble."

Political Discontent and Opposition

In the 1970s, two opposition movements were formed to create change, the Movement for Justice in Africa and the Progressive Alliance of Liberians (PAL). The Movement for Justice in Africa was committed to working toward social equality in the long term, but was not as aggressive in its political rhetoric as the PAL (Rinehart 1985). The PAL was committed to a critique of its class-based society. It demanded more immediate and drastic change in the government (Matthews 1980). The PAL became quite instrumental in the downfall of the Americo-Liberian government, though the course of events took an unfortunate, and unforeseen, turn.

In 1979, the minister for agriculture proposed an increase in the price of rice. A one hundred pound bag of rice, then sold at a subsidized price of 22 USD, would be raised to US$26, increasing the profit for farmers, and encouraging them to continue to work the fields rather than leaving their farms to look for wage labor in the city or on rubber plantations (Rinehart 1985). However, President William Tolbert (who had succeeded Tubman in 1971) had come under increasing criticism for corruption. That Tolbert's family was in the business of large-scale rice farming and stood to benefit substantially from the price increase did not escape the notice of the PAL. A march on the Executive Mansion was organized to protest the price increase in one of Liberia's most staple foods. Some 2,000 unarmed students and other citizens turned out. The government panicked and sent police to stop the march.

The protestors would not stand down. When tear gas failed to stop them, the police opened fire and rioting and looting ensued (Liebenow 1985). The 1979 Rice Riots turned out to be the tipping point after more than a century of exclusion and differential incorporation. Two days before the trial of the opposition leaders, Tolbert's rule came to an abrupt end.

A successful coup attempt saw Samuel Doe become the first indigenous head of state. Doe's regime was characterized by fear, suspicion, and liberal use of the machine gun (Sawyer 1992). Unfortunately, he continued the pattern of favoritism and exclusion of his elite predecessors. Doe decreed that thirteen elite government officials be publicly killed on the beach, an event that has become known as "The Beach Party" (Reno 1998). Americo-Liberians fled the country while the Krahn and Mandingo ethnic groups enjoyed privileged access to economic and educational opportunities denied to others. These and other events precipitated multiple coup attempts by excluded ethnic groups, all of which failed. The subsequent discrimination against these tribes caused an abundance of interethnic tension within Liberia (Outram 1997).

Doe's regime was immensely corrupt, siphoning millions off of the government for private patronage in the years following his takeover. Large formal sector exporters began to leave in the 1980s, which resulted in a significant decline of export earnings (Reno 1998). This era of "unparalleled brutality" (Levitt 2005) was brought to a close by a man who claimed ethnic and elite origins (Harris 1999) and an army that espoused no ethnic agenda (Outram 1997).

Civil War

On Christmas Eve in 1989, Charles Taylor and 168 trained soldiers invaded Nimba County from the Ivory Coast. The National Patriotic Front of Liberia (NPFL) attacked government troops, and from there quickly recruited hundreds of Liberians for the cause of overthrowing Doe's government, initiating a new phase of brutality that lasted for over a decade. When the war did not end after the assassination of President Doe in 1990, it became apparent that Taylor was waging war not to overthrow a corrupt leader, but to establish himself as the country's head of state (Moran 2006). He was trained as a "revolutionary" under Muammar Gaddafi, and his military campaign was neither marked with the exclusion of prior elite governments nor the ethnic favoritism of Doe's leadership. However, his political agenda turned out to be more of what Vigh (2006a) refers to as a "rebellion" than a revolution. The objective was to change the players, rather than to address the structural inequalities that caused the unrest in the first place. Numerous groups sprang up to challenge Taylor's quest for state power. The Economic Community of West African States agreed to deploy the Economic Community of West African States Monitoring Group (ECOMOG), a joint military intervention force. ECOMOG moved in to protect parts of the city and the government administration in Monrovia.

During the years between 1990 and 1996 Taylor's forces took over most of Liberia, controlling nearly 90 percent of the territory outside of Monrovia, and leveraging the nation's resources for their military aims (Reno 1998). The NPFL launched multiple attacks on Monrovia during that time in an attempt to overthrow the Armed Forces of Liberia and the ECOMOG troops stationed as guardians of the state capital. A group known as United Liberation Movement of Liberia (ULIMO) mobilized and fought with ECOMOG and the Armed Forces of Liberia against Taylor, later splintering into two groups, one under Roosevelt Johnson (ULIMO-J), and the other under Ahlaji Kromah (ULIMO-K). In 1996 there was a ceasefire, and in July 1997 elections were held. Charles Taylor won by a landslide, with most observers attributing the victory to his military dominance and the fear of the people. The interwar years (1997–1999) were marked by tension and unrest. Organized armed conflict resumed in 1999, this time with Taylor cornered in Monrovia, and LURD (Liberians United for Reconciliation and Democracy) and MODEL (Movement for Democracy in Liberia) controlling approximately 70 percent of Liberia (Waugh 2011). In 2003 Taylor finally relinquished his power in Liberia and accepted asylum in Nigeria (Levitt 2005).

Throughout the book, I have chosen to follow the lead of Liberians like Darlington, who refer to "the civil war" as the entire period of fourteen years between 1989 and 2003. I have made this semantic choice because the country remained tense throughout the fragile "peace" in the late '90s, and because this was how the Liberians in my work chose to refer to it. Other scholars choose to refer to the First Civil War (1989–1996) and the Second Civil War (1999–2003). This is also accurate, and a choice made by acknowledging the cease-fire and the first DDR initiative that were all subsumed in the return to fighting in 1999.

The harm caused during the war was immense. Estimates suggest that the death toll was extreme, numbering somewhere between 300,000 and 500,000 between 1989 and 2003 (see McMullin 2013, 66). An estimated 750,000 Liberians fled their homes (UN 2013). The infrastructure suffered from disrepair, with roads left to deteriorate as the war dragged on. Notably, the hydroelectric power plant that supplied electricity to the urban capital was damaged beyond use, leaving the city to function on generators.

What began as a project to transplant unwanted people from the United States grew into a country where a dominant minority elite built a state on the premises of exclusion and deferential incorporation. For the Americo elite, being in but not of Africa proved an impossible position to maintain (Ciment 2013). They mortgaged the resources of their country to foreign corporations who extracted them for foreign profit. As the oppression mounted, the gateway to civil war became more and more vulnerable to collapse.

Observing the exclusion of the indigenous majority by the Americos, Bøås (2001) argues that the war was in large part the result of neopatrimonial rule, a form of personal rule originally taken from Weber (1978), in which the leader seeks to acquire and ensure the well-being of his own group. It is "neo" in that such personal politics have been adapted to function within formal institutions. Bøås suggests that by redistributing resources among themselves, and by cultivating a pejorative and condescending view of the "other" (the indigenous communities), the Americos set the country on a course that was simply untenable in the long-term. His assessment of the social and structural developments over time is a welcome addition in the midst of numerous ahistorical theorizations that put civil wars down to greed (Collier and Hoeffler 2004), feasibility (Collier, Hoeffler, and Rohner 2006), or demographic imbalance (Urdal 2004. 2006). The Americos' negative view and treatment of the indigenous majority is uncontested by historians. However, if we leave it at neopatrimonial rule by the elite minority in Liberia, the interpretation remains a country-centric one. The earliest colonization efforts in the United States, which began the settlements that grew into the country of Liberia, were rooted in racist exploitation that led to civil war in the United States, and that could only culminate in the sorts of structural violence observed throughout the history of the Liberian nation. The country of Liberia grew out of an attempt to export the enormous and unwieldy implications of the slave trade, and in so doing, transplanted the abjection of the less "civilized" in the United States to the shores of the West African coast.

The young men in this book have inherited the implications of that initiative. Their life chances are severely restricted because their lives, and the lives of their forefathers, mattered less than those of the dominant cultural fraction in their country, and in the international arena beyond their borders. Appropriations of young men as irrationally violent and prone to destruction reify the underlying prejudice at work in the New Barbarism, and hark back to the fundamental ideologies that fueled the brutality of the slave trade. In so doing, the loose molecules paradigm scapegoats young people as causes for wars, conveniently obscuring the dominance and actions of international and regional forces that shape inequalities and marginalize huge numbers of people. My aim in this chapter is to set the analytical lens wide enough to expose the structural violence that led to the war, so that the young participants depicted in this book might be understood as much more than exotic, aggressive, and uncivilized young black men—a racist thread in international discourse that is remarkably persistent and enormously destructive.

3

Reciprocity, Respect, and Becoming Established

The damage done by the war was immense and multifaceted. Roads were badly damaged and that made travel slow and uncomfortable. Schools and medical facilities were understaffed, undersupplied, and not nearly numerous enough to provide care for the urban population. City lights had only just been restored to a small, central grid of the urban capital when I began fieldwork in 2010. Even then, a government official remarked candidly to me that the city and the country were not really in "reconstruction," they were in recovery. Young people felt the lack of opportunities acutely. While the scholarship around young people often focuses on the diminished opportunities experienced by a youthful generation, in the case of the young men in Liberia, their parent's generation was hit equally hard.

"There were jobs before. There aren't jobs," Andrew commented one evening in the yard. He was a good friend and a thoughtful guide to my understanding of his country. We had been talking about his experience of growing up during the war and his observations about how the country changed for the people since it ended. "It wasn't like that before the war, Abby. Really, it wasn't like that. Like for myself, my dad worked in the mines. We had a big compound. Everybody's parents were working there. They had what they needed. . . . But, now, parents aren't able."

Like Andrew's parents, many people were employed by foreign companies like Firestone or Liberian-American-Swedish Minerals

Company. Shortly after the war began in 1989 the vast majority of transnational corporations shut down or severely reduced operations in Liberia. Most had been slow to return and reopen, or had not come back at all at the time of this research. The physical and economic destruction that was levied on the country resulted in significant losses for families and households. Money, material possessions, and property were damaged, destroyed, or taken during the years of conflict. Many young people lost their parents to death or separation during the war, which meant that they were out on their own, hustling like Darlington. This chapter explores the structure of support as it was meant to unfold through intergenerational reciprocity, so that the loss of a helping hand can be more fully understood.

During my fieldwork my home was in Central Matadi, nestled on a curve in the road, under a line of big trees that shaded the yard from the afternoon sun. As the weeks went by I found myself frequenting one of the many stands where young men changed money (Liberian and US currency mostly) and sold top-up phone credit, or "scratch cards" as they are called. I usually went to Stephen's stand because he was always there, no matter the time of day. Tucked under a bright, multicolored umbrella, Stephen could be found leaning on the caged box where he kept his stacks of currency, bound tight with rubber bands, or sitting just behind it in a short plastic lawn chair. He was wily, as many survivalists are. He cheated me out of change once. I returned to engage in a somewhat playful exchange of banter, an interaction in which I was the decided loser, and he kept the miscounted change he had taken in his favor. Stephen was nearly always surrounded by a small posse of young men. They sat with him to pass the time, read the newspaper, talk about football, and comment on the passersby.

On a slow afternoon I sat down with him and listened to his views of the country and his thoughts about the future.

"A lot of people have to live in the area," he said, referring to the neighborhood. "They rent. They don't have a house of their own. They don't have the means, so they are just renting. They're not investing for themselves, they just rent. You see some guys around here, they might be thirty or forty years old, and they are not established."

"What do you mean by established?" I asked.

"If someone is established, they might have their own house. They have a way of getting money. They have their family all around them, their children are in school. A lot of people are not established for themselves. It's difficult, it's difficult. . . . As for me, my own parents were killed. My mother and my father were killed during the war. I have to make an effort. There is nobody to help me. I have to make an effort for myself. I graduated from high school in 2002. Since then, I haven't been able to do anything. Eight years, and I haven't been able to do anything, really."

At thirty-three years old, he was not established, and still very much a "youth." Despite his frustration, by comparison with so many of the young men in Monrovia, his conditions were relatively comfortable. At some point he had gotten work in private security, saved a little bit of money, and with the help of a patron, started his money changing and scratch card business on the side of the road. He rented a room, hoped to attend the University of Liberia one day, and took care to look after his siblings and remaining relatives when he could.

"I have two little sisters and one little brother, and I have to keep them in mind," he said. "I have other relatives as well. If they need a little something, if they need help with school fees, they come to me. I don't give them everything, but I give them something to try to help them out."

Stephen's inability to transition into a more established social and economic status is a plight he shares with young people, especially young men, around the world. In the literature youth are predominantly cast as a generation collectively thwarted from achieving status as adults. Their feelings of frustration with inhibited or foreclosed transitions take the foreground (see Jeffrey 2010b; Langevang 2008; Mains 2012; McDowell 2003; Utas 2005a). In some instances, environments have become so depleted that authors like Vigh (2006b) refer to youth as a "social moratorium," and in Jeffrey's (2010a) estimation, a permanent social condition for some. Substantial and insightful work has sought to locate and understand youth transitions within shifting political and economic structures that enable and inhibit their ability to make a living or to gain an education (Ferguson 1999; Furlong and Cartmel 2007; Jeffrey 2010b; Mains 2012; Vigh 2006a). This body of work situates the struggle to transition or survive within macro-level analyses of neoliberal economic reform, the false value of formal education, or chronic political instability that prohibits youth agency toward "established" lives. This is perhaps one of the reasons why familial networks of support are often omitted from the literature on youth. In the midst of challenging and informing the failure of large political and economic structures to support the young, there has been less attention given to the immediate social supports that remain essential to young people's everyday lives and social standing.

Within this literature "navigation" has become a dominant and trendy metaphor invoked by scholars who use the term to describe youth agency in rapidly shifting socioeconomic situations (Furlong 2009, 2013). Navigation, Vigh (2006a) argues, is able to capture a tactical exercise of negotiating immediate circumstances while maintaining focus on future possibilities and destinations. Though this agentive exercise may explicitly include navigating social relationships, as in Vigh's work, the attention usually remains on the individual's pursuit of opportunities and status, and we lose sight of their interconnectedness with families, kinship structures, or their broader communities. Part of this tendency is bound up in the liminal transition period of being a "youth," which is often synonymous with movement outside of family households as well as migration beyond home communities. Young people are not physically with their parents, their siblings, or their wider kin relations. Their movements away from "hearth and home" tend to draw attention to their individual transitions and trajectories. My contention in this book is that family support systems are often more present and fundamental than they appear in much of the literature. When they are absent or unavailable, a neoliberal bias toward emphasis on the individual prevents us from appreciating how significant the loss of reciprocity in family and kin networks really is.

The following sections illustrate how obligations in hierarchical social relations formed the primary supports for young people's life chances, transitions, and trajectories. As Chabal (2009, 48) writes, "The web of obligations that link people is densest at the core of the kinship association and more diffuse at its periphery." The chapter demonstrates how reciprocity works in families and households to facilitate youth transitions and the achievement of honor and prestige. It serves as a foundation that allows us to better understand how significant these webs of obligations in kin networks really are, so that the challenge of living life without them, as Stephen and so many young people were, can be more fully appreciated. It also points to the postwar reemergence of structural power dynamics depicted in the history chapter. Young men's imagined futures indicate a continuation of value for Americo-elite culture and jobs in government, suggesting that the war has not caused significant disruption to a long-lasting pattern of value for assimilation into the dominant cultural fraction.

Webs of Obligation

The time and energy required to feed, clothe, shelter, and support young people's transitions through childhood and toward adulthood was a collective, intergenerational effort among members of the household, family, and kin. Certainly, there could be important patrons outside of familial relations (see Bledsoe 1990); however, those who were most obligated were connected through kinship. Before I go any further, I should articulate how I am using these terms about family and kinship. In this work I use "family" to designate immediate relations such as parents, siblings, spouses, and children—the "nuclear" family, as they are known in the West. Wider kinship networks are those extending outward to in-laws, grandparents, cousins, aunties, and uncles. This is my semantic choice, made to establish a sense of degrees of proximity within hierarchical webs of obligation. It is by no means a fixed category.

"Family" as a term of reference was used quite broadly by Liberians to indicate all manner of kinship and fictive kin. Though there were significant expectations around reciprocity to one's immediate family—for instance, to take care of aging parents—households were often composed of all manner of kinship ties, and the day-to-day reciprocity between them usually fell along gerontocratic lines, where younger members were expected to serve their elders.

Bledsoe's (1980) work with the Kpelle in Liberia has been particularly useful to my theoretical understanding of young men's life chances in Monrovia. Wealth in people is a form of social organization that functions through control of others. Traditionally, these hierarchical relations have been gendered, with men in positions of social dominance over women, and gerontocratic, with elders asserting control over younger persons. Among the Gola in Liberia d'Azevedo (1962) observed that every male adult was a patron to a "lesser person," such as women and children, and a client to others. Though I believe that we may observe some challenge to these elements of hierarchical structure, particularly as women take greater responsibilities as breadwinners in the urban environment, most Liberians, adults and youth alike, were embedded in kinship networks that were still more or less structured around gender and generation.

Unlike theories of social capital (see Lin 1999; Putnam 1995), in a system of wealth in people social relations are not merely helpful connections that assist personal development or socioeconomic mobility—they are literally the means to these ends. "Labor and allegiance," Bledsoe (1980, 48) writes, "are critical to people's economic subsistence as well as to their political and economic advancement. Wealth and security rest on the control of others." In Sierra Leone, Shaw (2000) traces the significance of wealth in people to agricultural reproduction and to the slave trade. At that time the successful cultivation of crops depended on the capacity of a farmer to control the labor of others, something that was accomplished through accruing ties of dependency and indebtedness in kinship, marriage, parenthood, or fosterage. Circumstances precipitated by the slave trade required that groups be armed for warfare to protect their people from slave-raiding posses, and leaders built a following of supporters whose security depended on them. They in turn provided services that would support the protection and well-being of the group. In such contexts, independence or individual isolation from a group was dangerous. It was through belonging to and with others that one found security (Kopytoff and Miers 1977).

The role of patrons and patronage remains important for social systems throughout Africa, and Liberia is no exception. Though patronage is often observed within political contexts of leadership and authority—as with leaders who acquired the allegiance of warriors during the slave trade—it is also exercised within households. Interdependence through patronage is vital to survival and well-being in the every day as well as in the long term. Goody (1982) observes that the act of rearing a child creates a debt that the child is expected to pay back. The training, provision, and protection that parents and other caregivers provide to their charges creates a debt that children must repay through their labor and allegiance.

In my household, children were the primary task force that kept the household running. There was rarely a lull in the hum of human activity around the house and in the yard. I usually awakened to the sound of a child sweeping outside, the coarse bristles of a broom brushing across the sand, gathering the trash that had blown into the yard during the night. Older children got the young ones ready for school. They dressed and fed them, reprimanded them when necessary—for whining, complaining, or dawdling. Mothers, aunties, and any other onlooking adults supervised the daily routines of the young household members. The patronage of the elders and their investment in the young ones was always near the surface of social interaction. I listened one afternoon as a mother in my yard slowly recounted the amount of money she had spent on her daughter's clothes, the school fees she had paid, reminding the noncompliant child of her duty to fulfill a command made by her mother, a woman who provided for her so thoroughly.

What might appear to some, at least at first, as an authoritarian and dominating role for older persons who were in positions over the younger ones is actually part of intergenerational interdependence, relationships that were far more reciprocal than might immediately meet the eye. These were relationships in which exchange and obligation in the mundane, everyday tasks laid the foundation of reciprocal support that would extend well into the future. Children were at the beck and call of their elders, but by fulfilling their obligations, the younger ones earned the right to make certain requests of them. If unmet, these requests would appear equally shameful for their older superiors. It would impinge on the bigger person's honor. As an older guest, I was tended to by one of the children in my household. She prepared my food every day and she earned the right to make a claim on reciprocity from me—occasionally requesting phone credit, chocolate "from town," or bootlegged DVDs sold by the road. I did my best to oblige and always felt a twinge of regret and shame if I did not meet her request.

Obligations between elder patrons and their younger dependents extend well into later life. Children are the primary source of social security in one's old age (Bledsoe 1980; Harrell-Bond 1975), and relations of intergenerational indebtedness are to be taken very seriously. My conversation with William illustrates how significant decisions to reciprocate in the immediate and short term could be for long-term security and well-being. William was a friend of my neighbors. We sat chatting with one another on an afternoon while he waited for someone to return to the house. He explained that he and his wife had two children together, and that his nineteen-year-old stepdaughter also lived in the household. He told me that he and his wife had experienced an enormous disagreement concerning her. It had reached such a fever pitch that he had left the household and chosen to live elsewhere for the past four months. His stepdaughter had gotten pregnant and had a child.

"No one to claim the child," he noted. This was a huge concern to Liberian parents and caregivers throughout my work, and it will resurface in fuller detail in the following chapter.

William related that his stepdaughter had frustrated him by not attending to her obligations to him. She did not respect her position in his household by contributing to the workload, by washing his clothes or taking care of things when he asked. He was feeding, clothing, and sheltering her, yet she failed to reciprocate, and had become pregnant with a second child, "another mouth to feed!" His frustration mounted with the second pregnancy, and tension escalated within the household.

"I got vexed," he noted. He fell out with his wife because she refused to support him when he made requests of his stepdaughter and the young one refused to oblige him. He eventually left the household in anger, and had only just returned when he sat down and began talking with me. He said that he had resolved to come back and work with his wife and stepdaughter to resolve the issue.

"I should take care of my children," he said. "If I don't, they won't be there for me in my old age."

William's struggle to maintain intergenerational reciprocity reflects the significance of being indebted to one's dependents. His experience also highlights how challenging it could be to maintain reciprocity, and build intergenerational interdependence. Ideally, fulfillment of roles and responsibilities strengthens reciprocal relationships. To have wealth in people is to have relationships in which obligations bind two or more parties together. The loyalty and labor of dependent children is contingent upon the provision and protection of their parents or guardians. Each must do their part for the other. Through the exchange of reciprocal obligations, each becomes increasingly indebted to the other.

What I have just described is a very functional arrangement of social exchange. As such, it might appear that there is never a "true" or altruistic gift, a point of extensive debate in anthropology, and one that harks back to early works by Malinowsky (1961) and Mauss (1950). Though Liberian households, families, and kin networks operated on an explicitly conditional and contingent form of intergenerational reciprocity, I do not mean to suggest that there were never gifts, services, or favors that were offered without expectation of return or as an outflow of love or care. Nor should we make the mistake of assuming that duties and responsibilities to reciprocate are devoid of affection or goodwill. Function and affection are not mutually exclusive (see Mains 2013). That said, I did not observe a pervasive exercise of what Sahlins (1965) coined "generalized reciprocity" within households. He suggests that households are microcosms in which the freest gifts are most often distributed without expectation of return. Though I am sure that such gifts were bestowed among and between members of the household, the majority of social exchange was part of immediate household reproduction and an investment in long-term well-being.

Respect through Reciprocity: An Example in Fosterage

These webs of obligations are intricately and intimately linked to achievement of respect—respect that Stephen's generation was desperate to achieve and found difficult to accomplish. I have chosen to make use of Spencer's (1965) distinction of respect as honor and respect as prestige. Though Iliffe (2005) dismisses Spencer's use of the two constructs, arguing that he has not seen them manifested in his extensive work on the continent, I find Spencer's work conceptually useful in the Liberian context. Liberians' prolific use of patronage in foster relationships provides an excellent example of these constructs in everyday life.

Child fosterage was one way to increase the number of dependents in a household—and therefore the number of indebted beneficiaries who would be obligated to their fostering patrons. Fosterage is a long-established practice in West Africa (Bledsoe 1990, 1993; Goody 1982; Isiugo-Abanihe 1985). Fostering children has been done to free parents for other responsibilities, to provide relatives, especially elderly ones, with domestic labor, and for social mobility of the young. Most homes with room and resources hosted one if not several foster children at once. Many received children from outside the city. In some cases, parents were deceased or unable to pay for children's education, and so they were sent to wealthier relatives in the urban area. In other instances, parents were alive but looked to relatives who could improve their children's life chances through access to better schools.

By hosting foster children, heads of house earned respect as both honor and prestige. Prestige, according to Spencer, is respect earned for rising above one's peers. Households with many dependents were noticed and recognized for having the resources to handle many people. In that way, they increased their prominence in the community. The more dependents in one's sphere of control, the more prestigious one's social standing became. For the households with the resources to do it, fostering children was also the *right* and *expected*—the honorable—thing to do. Relatives of lower socioeconomic status had the right to ask wealthier kin to foster a child. The honor of those who were able to offer a helping hand depended on providing for those who were less socially and economically established. Fosterage demonstrates how intertwined the two forms of respect often were. What was socially honorable led to greater prominence, to prestige. The more prestige won through rising above one's peers, the more dependents could make claims on obligations to support and provide.

Fosterage was contingent on reciprocity. All of the foster children I knew were incorporated into the household division of labor. Those who failed to comply with their hosts' wishes lost privileges. I saw multiple foster children lose the privilege to stay. A boy I knew was living with his aunty to attend a better school. He could be slow with his household tasks, and at times disobedient. He was sent back to his mother after several of these episodes occurred. Foster children who worked hard and were compliant earned honor in the eyes of their elders and increased their chances of benefiting from the favor they achieved.

Mobility through Patronage

Hierarchical webs of obligation channeled goods, services, and opportunities. It is essential that we position young men's struggle to become established within the context of these unequal and interdependent relations. The density and durability of their core networks of support determined how enabled and facilitated their transitions toward adulthood were. Their access to school fees or job opportunities was nearly always a function of their wealth in people. While we were talking beneath the umbrella at his stand, Stephen noted with frustration, "I just need the opportunity. That's the problem—one of the problems in this society. You know, some people they get a job, and then they get their families jobs there too. It's difficult. You don't have a job, and you don't have family to get you in."

Though it would be a challenge to substantiate how prolifically patronage networks, especially within kinship, were mobilized to keep opportunities flowing within personal webs of obligation, there was every indication that procuring a spot in school or in a job was largely a function of personal affiliations. Patrons were needed for fees, for introductions, and for placements.

Titus provides a helpful example of family systems and kinship relations that facilitated young men's transitions under relatively ideal circumstances—the kind of circumstances that most young men wanted, but very few seemed to have. A student at the University of Liberia, Titus presented a calm demeanor, noticeably lacking the edge of frustration I often picked up in conversations with Stephen and other young men. Both of Titus's parents had survived the war. They had two small dwellings that sheltered the household, which included his grandmother, little sister, both parents, and himself. His parents were able to help him with money if he needed clothes or supplies for school.

Hunched over a table in the upstairs library of the university, I asked Titus, "How did you wind up getting to come to school and so many others don't?"

"I don't pay tuition. The reason is because I'm on my grandfather. He's an employee here. . . . I'm benefiting from his employment. . . . Yeah, so that's how it come about."

A well-connected grandfather provided possibilities that young men like Stephen lacked.

"There's a very important word, Abby," Moses, a local pastor in Monrovia, noted, leaning across his desk. "'Interest.' Let's say you and I go for a job in the government. There is a big man there. Let's say you and I are equally qualified, or even, you are more qualified than me—but he says, 'I know the man. I have interest in him.' I will get the job, because he will say, 'I know that fellow.' That's how it works . . . they're protecting their own, individual interests."

Stephen described the redistribution of opportunities within family relations as "a problem" in society. It meant that young men like himself faced reduced options because their links to bigger people were few and because their primary support in parents had been diminished or was entirely gone. However, because of the social value of intergenerational reciprocity, for bigger people being in the position to facilitate a job placement or to redistribute opportunities among their dependents was a chance to increase respect as honor and prestige. They were providing for those to whom they were socially obligated, for whom it was their right and expected duty to help, while increasing their investment in dependents who were under their control.

Dependence was a "mode of action" (Ferguson 2013). Young people's ability to improve their economic or material wealth was inextricably connected to those upon whom they could call for favors, or lay claim to obligations. In this way, it is important to think about wealth in people as having people above and below one's position in the social strata. Having dependents under one's control increased status and security, but it was every bit as important to have others upon whom one could make claims.

Most youth that I knew were in Stephen's position. They were keen to improve their life chances through education and work but they lacked the wealth in people to acquire opportunities. Edwin was an exception. His social status and social relations provide a useful contrast, one that points to the salience of the class divide that persisted in the years following the war. Edwin was established. He had not chosen a wife, but he had the means to provide for one. He drove a car that had been brought over from America. Always clean, well groomed, and well spoken, he had a house and a job in the government.

"That's everybody's dream," Jake commented. Edwin had the comfort he hoped to achieve. "You have a job. You have money. You have a television in your house. You have your own machine generator, you know? You are living up to standard, you are living well."

As an established man, Edwin had achieved the dream. Though we were friendly with one another, it would have been far too personal to ask him about his patronage networks and his links to the government. However, the topic came up one evening over beers with a mutual friend of ours. I asked Tee about how Edwin had managed to acquire a position when so many young men his age were struggling. I noticed that he carried an Americo (Western) name, and asked her about it.

"His father was Americo," she replied. Edwin shared a surname with one of the most powerful and influential families in the country. "He had Edwin by an indigenous woman who could not speak English. Now Edwin uses his Western name to get the kind of job he has at the ministry."

Edwin's status through wealth in people reflects a historic and persistent class divide. Bledsoe (1980) provides an illustrative example of patronage in the decades prior to the war, of the kind of social connections that were now being reproduced among young men like Edwin in the postwar years. She tells the story of a young man named Dumu who was taken from his village in the interior to live with a high-ranking national leader. He lived in the household and was educated in exchange for his contribution of labor. He increased his status by becoming educated and having strong ties to the "civilized world." Politically, his father gained a useful relationship with the central government that could benefit him in the interior. Connections to bigger people improved life chances for the individual as well as their networks of dependents. In Edwin's case, his father increased political ties to the interior by marrying an indigenous woman. This gave Edwin a network of obligations to draw upon through his father in the urban center.

Big Men

The more prestige earned for rising above one's peers, the bigger the person. The top positions in social hierarchies were held by "big men" and a few "boss ladies," with the president at the time, Ellen Johnson Sirleaf, being chief among them. Big men and boss ladies held their positions of dominance by leveraging social relations to acquire and mobilize goods, labor, and services (see Sahlins 1963; Utas 2012). They had interest in and influence across many hierarchical webs of obligation.

While I was in Red Light, the market area that will fill the content of the following chapter, I asked some of the youth, "What does a big man look like?"

Pieced together from several interjections, they responded, "Big men ride in cars. They live in the fence. They don't want to expose what they have. Their house, maybe they have two or three cars. . . . They hold position. Most of them work in government. Other people work for them. They serve them. . . . When they come into the community (like Red Light), they come to be known. They want to be popular in the community. If they are good, they will help."

Their observation that most big men worked in the government always held true in my fieldwork. I never met or heard about a big man who did not hold a position of influence or power purely outside of the government. This was a pattern that had continued from the founding of the republic. Though they might have farms or other enterprises, the Americo minority elite made the business of government their top priority. In the postwar years, the government was again a primary seat of power. Big men were woven into the fabric of power relations within the state.

At one point, one of the young men in Red Light spoke up and said that he and all of his peers were looking for "somebody."

"You looking for someone to help you?" I asked him.

"Thank you!" he replied, affirming my correct response.

"Big man?"

"Thank you! Someone who can help me [so] I can sustain myself. In the future, I help him."

Everyone was looking for a person with power and influence who could improve their life chances and support their trajectories toward higher social status. Utas (2012) notices this as well, observing that people seek out and maintain ties to multiple big men in their quest for the benefits of protection, provision, or opportunity. Young men who did not have patronage through family, as Edwin did, looked to big men who were on the periphery of their core networks of obligations, and in some cases were outside of them altogether. For the big man, a significant part of maintaining the labor or services of his followers was to maintain popularity and leverage through demonstrations of wealth and goodwill, through largesse. They made displays of wealth as a means of demonstrating their prestige, and they redistributed resources of various kinds in order to maintain reciprocal relations with supporters who were under them.

In the postwar context, adulthood garnered respect as both honor and prestige. Socioeconomic establishment as an adult meant that young men were no longer depending on caregivers to support them, and could begin to provide for dependents. This was a socially honorable position that young men wanted to earn in the eyes of their family, kin, and communities. It positioned them well above most of their peers. It was also a difficult position for most to achieve in an environment where maintaining sustainable livelihoods with the resources to support a wife, children, or aging parents was impossible for many.

A Class Ceiling

As I listened to the youth talk about becoming established and looking for big men to help them, there was a common thread in their narratives that points to a resolidification of the class divide historically held by the urban, elite Americos. Nearly all of my informants aspired to jobs in the government. The elite minority of settlers established a clear pattern of choosing government opportunities rather than private sector employment. As the twentieth century progressed, the trend continued. Assimilation into urban elite culture meant looking for opportunities in the government rather than the private sector.

"We feel that the best way to success is to get to government by any means possible," Alex commented of his countrymen. "Steal from government, and get started. We don't feel that if you work hard in the private sector or in our own businesses, we can succeed. The only way to succeed is to force ourselves into government."

Alex's comments were made from the outside looking in to the government. From the inside, an upper-level employee of the Finance Ministry described the benefit of working for the government in similar terms. There were ways of stealing gas money on the government's tab or claiming expenses under the guise of state business. It was not that government jobs paid so well. It was that government jobs came with abundant opportunities to freeload on state money. This is how big men who worked in the higher positions of the government were able to pad their own pockets.

One of the biggest benchmarks of elite status was the human and cultural capital (Bourdieu 1986) that came in the form of a foreign educational degree, most often from the United States. Lower-level positions like Edwin's job provided opportunities to access government resources for personal gain. Though his elite affiliations, his position, and his material possessions placed him well above young men like Stephen in the social strata, I spent enough time with powerful elites in the city to know that his patronage and level of prestige was not enough to win him status as a big man. The biggest men and women had lived and been educated in developed countries, most often in the United States.

There is a long tradition of elite migration to the United States for education. A large proportion of the ruling minority of elite men received university degrees from colleges and universities in the United States (Liebenow 1962). Elite money and wealth in people in the United States made these options possible. The same pattern was evidenced in government officials and repatriated elites I knew during fieldwork. They hailed from universities such as Columbia, George Mason, Harvard, or the University of Wisconsin. Some members of this group were displaced with their families when Samuel Doe took over in the coup in 1980. In their case, forced migration laid the foundation for pursuing American education.

Reference, resemblance, and affiliation with the United States produced a significant cultural capital among the elite. To have a U.S. credential was of significant worth among the ruling class. What was on "that side" in America was considered more civilized, and what was civilized was considered more sophisticated, and hence more valuable.

"Yeah, on that part of Liberian history," Jake noted. "What I read and what I see, only those that came from over there with degree, from Harvard University, from Oxford University, you know? England, Germany, you will find most of them working. But you come from University of Liberia with BSE or master's, no one will see you [and] carry on serious—any of them you see. Any of them you see going and coming back have position."

Those who were not of elite origin themselves often benefited from elite connections to the United States. President Johnson Sirleaf has said her education in the United States was enabled through the elite affiliations she possessed among family members (Johnson Sirleaf 2009). Her own education includes a bachelor's degree from the University of Colorado at Boulder and a graduate degree from Harvard University. I met other, far less famous individuals who pursued bachelor's and graduate degrees in a similar fashion. Although not all of them could boast the Ivy League clout of Harvard or Yale, it was a stateside degree more than an Ivy League credential that was so important.

Though Western, U.S. credentials were not necessarily the only indicator of elite prestige, they were a noticeable symbol of status that separated the ruling class from everyone else. The young men in this work made it abundantly clear that while pursuing a university degree or vocational training certificate in Liberia was better than nothing, it was not good enough to become a big man. The likelihood that it would provide lasting improvement to one's situation was dubious. It was better to "go on that side," where your chances were more certain afterwards.

One morning I shared a taxi with a smiley young man who congenially commented, "We don't even respect our own degree. If you come with a degree from University of Liberia and someone else comes with a degree from America they will give it to the man with the degree from America." This issue was pressing on the young people, he asserted. It was better to leave the country and go somewhere else than to remain, because their progress would be slower than those who went to America and came back.

Young people from elite families that journeyed abroad and back again could establish comfortable lives in Monrovia. There are two further observations to make concerning migration to the United States. One is that the war opened a pathway for migration to the United States for a large cohort of nonelite Liberians who were granted access as refugees. What had been an elite privilege became a possibility for others. My informants knew many people who had gone over to the United States because of the war. Some had done well, gotten jobs and education, and were able to send remittances back to their family. There were far fewer stories of families coming back to Liberia. There were even fewer stories of nonelite Liberians taking jobs in higher positions of the government. However, most of those who came back as big men to "hold positions" were from elite backgrounds. On the other hand, it was very common to find nonelite young men who had gotten into trouble in the United States and been deported, losing the educational and economic opportunities that were so sought after "on that side." In short, the notion of going to the States to achieve something to return with was prevalent. However, the ability to achieve the privilege of prestige as a big man in the government seemed to remain with those of elite pedigree.

Conclusion

This chapter illustrates how goods, services, and opportunities were channeled through patronage, especially patronage within family and kinship networks. Familial relations were extraordinarily important for youth transitions and life chances. Having made this argument, I do not wish to present a romanticized notion of families as ideal, catch-all, or fix-all solutions to the "social moratorium" of youth. William's difficulty with his own family demonstrates that intergenerational reciprocity can be a challenge to maintain, and that when family relations are present, it is not a guarantee that reciprocity will follow and inevitably lead to well-being of any kind. What I am suggesting is that in the Liberian social structure, family and kin had the deepest and most enduring obligations to offer support. Patrons could also be found outside of the family. Bledsoe (1990) is clear on this point in Sierra Leone, and I did see indications of this in my own fieldwork. We had a young man who began spending time at our house, working on small projects for my host mother. She took an interest in him, and wanted to help. She became a patron for him, supporting his basic needs while he worked for her. Should push come to shove, however, her obligations to support the needs of her own children and her immediate family would always come first. Though she genuinely wanted to provide for this young man, and was increasing her prestige in doing so, his labor and allegiance were not nearly as important as those of her own family and kin.

Transitions into adulthood were significantly thwarted, and without personal affiliations to bigger people, most youth were relatively immobile. Stephen, like Darlington, could provide for himself but was unable to carry any dependents of his own. Livelihoods in the informal urban economy supported many young people in this way. They provided enough to subsist, but not nearly the means to become established.

Frustrated socioeconomic transitions among youth were in large part the result of the economic and material damage caused to their parents' and kinship networks during the war. Systems of support were significantly depleted of land, money, resources, and big people to provide patronage to their dependents. Webs of obligation lost their capacity to carry the extensive networks of patronage that facilitated youth transitions into established lives as adults. The implications of losing family and kinship obligations will be more fully explored in the following chapter.

Young men's perspectives about earning prestige as big men in government reflect a reproduction of social values that has its roots in the very beginning of the country. What was modern, Western, and from the United States was more valuable. The consolidation of the ruling class's power over the indigenous majority was maintained in large part through the maintenance of their own networks, and on the basis of difference in "cultural style" (Ferguson 1999) and the achievement of human capital from the United States. Positions of power in the government were kept to their class of people, while the rest of the country was co-opted and kept down.

The young men in this chapter did not voice opposition to these structural barriers, but rather, as their forefathers had done for so many generations leading up to the war, they sought to accommodate the demands of the dominant—to assimilate to their civilized culture and to achieve status by acquiescing to their norms and values. The historical struggle for dignity was being reproduced in the postwar terrain. As Jensen (2008) observes, as long as someone else—someone dominant—sets the criteria upon which social worth is conferred, it will remain largely out of reach. The reemergence of a structural class divide has implications for how we understand the postwar recovery of the nation, and will be discussed again more broadly in the conclusion in chapter 7.

4
Street Youth
Life on the Periphery

Wealth in people was vital to security and status. Historically this form of social organization emerged in circumstances where people were understood as scarce and valuable (Ferguson 2013). Yet in Liberia, as elsewhere on the continent, people are in surplus and much less valuable as laborers. Hierarchical webs of obligation have not been able to carry the weight of so many dependents. This chapter illustrates how a lack of bigger people manifested in the lives of a group of street youth. Most had lost supportive elders to death or displacement. For those whose parents and kin remained alive and accessible, their ability to provide for dependents had been significantly reduced by their loss of resources in things and people. Some young men like Darlington and Stephen were able to hustle for themselves enough to make a living. Many others wound up on the street.

Kaplan (1996) describes "hordes" of young men, everywhere, in multiple West African cities, restless and aggressive. I arrived in Monrovia prepared to reject such pejorative appropriations made about young black men. However, I was struck by how many young men were visibly scattered throughout my neighborhood, along the streets in the urban center, and in most places in the city. This chapter provides an account of those to whom the loose molecules paradigm is most often applied, and whose life chances bear the most resemblance to those of young ex-combatants who had little wealth in people after war.

Timothy was twenty-six years old when I met him. He spent every day in Red Light, one of the busiest markets in the Monrovia area. He passed the time with a few friends at a small shelter behind the market stalls, just beyond the congestion and noise of the car traffic. Days were passed talking, sleeping, smoking cigarettes and marijuana. Some occasionally found day labor hauling sand or laying cement blocks. Several, like Timothy, bought and sold small quantities of marijuana (which is technically illegal). Though their personal lives were all unique, what brought them all to the street was what Darlington emphasized that afternoon on the beach, the helping was not there.

I went to visit the youth in Red Light often, sitting to discuss their views on politics or their experiences of looking for work. We smoked cigarettes in the shade and watched the petty traders pass by, heavy-laden with bags or boxes stuffed with clothes, sheets, shoes, and any other item that could be sold, reused, or repurposed. Sometimes I walked with someone, so that we could talk away from the group, and listened to personal stories of surviving in their depleted postwar context. Timothy was the first youth that I got to know. A leader among his small community of friends in the market, he became something of a guide for me as I listened and learned about the hustle and flow of life lived on the periphery of core webs of obligation.

The everyday lives of these young people offer a challenge to some of the pejorative connotations linked to street youth among their communities and within academic and policy discourse. Liberians frequently disparaged the state of the country, and used the young people who were "on the street" as an indicator of hard times and the implications of the war that were yet to be rectified. Though everyone agreed that youth being on the street was a negative thing, sometimes it was hard to discern what that actually meant. Liberians bemoaned the lack of education and the way the young people's lives were wasting away without proper opportunities. Young men were highly visible on the streets, and many of them were not only unemployed but also relatively unoccupied. Yet there was also an element of disdain and stigma at times, as if being on the street was something especially harmful, associated with drugs, theft, or gang activity.

"What does it mean to be 'on the street'?" I asked Timothy.

"It means that you don't have parents in your life," he replied. "They might be alive, but you have left their house, their care. When you get up in the morning, you go on the street, and your activities probably revolve around drugs. You doing small jobs to support the habit, or dealing to support your habit and that of your friends."

Smoking marijuana was a regular fixture of everyday life for most of the young men in his network of support. It became a crucial means of "small money" for Timothy, which will become plain as his story unfolds. More central to his life story and to those of his friends is the first part of what he said. "It means you don't have parents in your life . . . you have left their house, their care." What defined the life chances of the young men I knew in Red Light was their lack of support in networks of obligation among family and kin. For reasons that were specific to each one's story, their ties of mutual dependence among family relations had been significantly weakened or completely severed, leaving them to struggle for survival outside of their core networks of obligation—which meant living or at least hustling on the street. Timothy is our guide through this chapter. Through his story, and with interjections from the voices of his friends, we see the implications of losing intergenerational reciprocity and witness the struggle "to make life" at the periphery of those networks. Within that struggle, stigma emerges as a prominent theme for these young men who hustle to survive the strain of survival on the streets.

Losing Reciprocal Obligations at the Core

In the years during and following the war, families and households were disrupted. Nearly everyone's story featured a steady progression of loss—both of people and of things. As Flomo, a member of the Elders Council of West Point, said, "Now, due to the poverty that affected the parents, it make it that we cannot meet up with our children's needs. And because of this, and they too are trying, one way or the other, to sustain themselves." Most had been internally or externally displaced during the fighting. Some were pushed into areas within Monrovia, where the Economic Community of West African States set up secured camps. Others were taken across borders into Ghana, Guinea, Ivory Coast, Nigeria, and Sierra Leone. Timothy's mother took him and his brother to Ivory Coast. There, as a refugee, he completed his high school education. When the war ended, the family moved back to Liberia, to Nimba County in the northeast. His mother and father were separated during the war, and afterwards his father was not able to support the family. A few years later his father died.

Timothy's mother was unable to offer much help, and was obligated to support younger family members. "You know, she's a poor woman," he related. "She has nothing much. And you know . . . it's like I was a burden on her too. She got three children with her. But that's other people's children she's catering to." Often, parents in poorer households were not able to cater to (support) their older, male children. Younger siblings and girls were considered more vulnerable, and foster children needed the support. Nearly everyone was facing depreciated circumstances while dealing with immediate and unrelenting needs. With no father and his mother unable to help him further, Timothy looked to an uncle who had moved to the United States. His uncle agreed to send money back to sponsor Timothy's education at a technical school in Monrovia. With the financial means to continue school, Timothy moved from Nimba County to a community outside of Monrovia to begin an engineering course.

The challenge that surfaced immediately was that Timothy did not "have people" in Monrovia. There was no kin relation with whom he could stay. There would be no children to cook a midday meal. No small girls or boys to do the washing and buying, no mat and no roof to share with others who could look out for his well-being, his security, or any other needs. As an isolated individual, the mundane everyday stress of living alone in the city quickly became difficult to manage.

"He [his uncle] was paying my fees, but not my bills," he explained. "As a young man, I went to school, I got plenty necessities . . . Clothing, shelter, food, and things—yeah, and you know it was kind of tough on me."

Unable to find a place to stay close to the school, Timothy found a manageable rent thirty minutes away. This meant that in addition to the monetary costs of food and shelter, he faced the additional time, money, and stress associated with transportation in the city. Commuting took a significant amount of energy in the overcrowded vehicles that traversed the rough, unrepaired roads. I learned how daunting it could be to "fight for car!" Motorbike taxis were readily available, but they were always twice as expensive as the car taxis that followed standard routes through the urban landscape. At peak times of the morning and evening large clusters of expectant people stood at heavily trafficked junctions, ready to throw elbows and hips in the way of anyone who challenged their prospects of a spot in a car. Taxis were packed so full of human bodies that it was often a chore to get the doors closed. It was indeed something of a fight to catch a ride, and one that could take an hour or more at the busiest parts of the day.

"I started dropping on my grades," he remembered. "And I couldn't study on time because you go and come from school—when you come from school, no food. You won't study."

Just attending to basic needs of everyday life took quite a bit of energy. The time-consuming, routine tasks of finding and preparing food would have to be handled on his own. The only alternative would be a cook shop or "street food." Either was convenient, but both were more expensive. Additionally, there were all sorts of hidden costs associated with attending school. Notebooks and writing utensils were only the beginning. Many instructors sold their lecture notes, without which it was difficult to pass exams. There were few textbooks, which meant that students had to make copies of reading materials because there were not enough books to go around. This too cost money. It was equally common for teachers and professors to take "small money" (bribes) for grades. All of these expenses compounded the cost of education. Timothy's uncle had not taken these expenditures into account.

"The man don't understand it from that perspective. He want me to just go to school. Going to school now, there are plenty things involved in school. You won't just pay the fee and enter the classroom just like that. I couldn't cope. When I call [my uncle] I try to explain things to him. You know, things are hard on this side in Liberia. We're just from war and no work for me. So if he really want to be helping me, let him send me some money . . . so I can be sustaining myself while going to school. But he never understood it from that point of view."

Unable to manage the stressors of solo existence in the city, Timothy eventually dropped out of his engineering course. When his uncle heard that he had dropped out, he resolved to try again to provide a helping hand. He committed to sponsor Timothy's fees out of an obligation to his nephew. It would have infringed upon his honor in front of the family to decline Timothy's needs. "You won't easily say 'no,'" as one woman put it to me. Social honor was contingent on fulfilling responsibilities to dependents. The obligation to act as a patron and to support those at the core of one's network was a responsibility taken seriously. However, from his position in the States, Timothy's uncle could not directly verify that Timothy was abiding by his expectations to use the money for school and living expenses, and suspected that Timothy might be squandering the funds in unnecessary ways. As a result, he chose to send the money through a male relative who was entrusted to mediate the monetary transaction between himself and his nephew. The man sent Timothy's school bill to his uncle in the States and received the money from his uncle to pay for his fees. This too became complicated.

"His only responsibility was to tell [my uncle], say, 'this is the bill.' And when he pay it, say 'here is the receipt,' scan the receipt and send it. I would tell him, 'I'm a technical student, I need so, so, and so tool.' He would tell me, 'it much.' When he writing [to my uncle], he won't tell him these things . . . So when he not [telling him], I kept my uncle informed."

Timothy's uncle had started this new mediated arrangement because of insufficient trust in Timothy's word. Now, sufficiently convinced that his intermediary was misrepresenting Timothy's circumstances, his uncle decided to send money directly to Timothy behind the relative's back. When the man became aware of the communication transpiring between Timothy and his uncle in the United States, he was angry. He called a family meeting, and questioned Timothy's honor in front of his relatives.

"He said that I can even be killing. Why? Because I can be doing something behind him. So you see, it got me downhearted. . . . He started saying plenty things about me to people. How in fact, I had undermined him. . . . Problems started coming from the family . . . so I myself decided to stop school."

Life on the Periphery

With the loss of his uncle's support and his reputation tarnished, Timothy found himself at a turning point. He would have to support himself one way or another, and there were no more obligations to tap for material support in his core network.

"I went to my mother in Nimba," Timothy said. "I went there and explained things to her. I spent two months with her and I came back." He had no means of contributing to the household in Nimba, and would be, as he put it, "a burden on her" if he chose to stay. Inability to engage in reciprocities within the household meant that young men like Timothy became financial drains to their families. It was difficult to justify staying in a household without the ability to contribute. In Timothy's case, when he left his mother's house in Nimba, he returned to Monrovia with few prospects and no money.

"From Nimba, I came back. . . . Really, at the time, I had nothing doing. And you know I never wanted to find myself in the streets jacking (stealing) phones. Once you on the streets you just gotta do something to get money. You're forced to get money to sustain yourself. Yeah, so one of my friends encouraged me. He had a little money. He took me, he carry me. That's how I started selling [marijuana] at first. From there, that's how I started selling for myself."

Liberians talk about parents "turning their children loose" because they do not want to care for them. They speak regretfully about impoverished parents who allow their children to run rampant in the streets. "There are parents who don't care," a man said to me. "They just born the child. That's a problem in Liberia."

It was a common view, one also reflected in early literature that constructed "street children" and "street youth" as runaways from family breakdowns and the implications of severe poverty (see Ennew and Swart-Kruger 2003). The National Youth Policy adopted similarly reductionist—even demeaning terms—stating that street youth were those who "lack any protection supervision or direction from responsible adults" (Ministry of Youth and Sports 2005, 9). There certainly were neglectful parents. However, neglect was not always the reason young people ended up on the street. Many young men like Timothy still had an open connection to family. They did not leave because they were put out or because they were not cared for. Often, their reasons were related to the financial strain on their families, and under those circumstances, transitioning out was more honorable than continuing to stay.

Timothy was fortunate enough to have a friend in the city who was willing to help him make a sustainable living. Most of his friends were less fortunate. Washington's experience of moving onto the street illustrates how demanding the hustle to find "daily bread" could be. When he had exhausted any chance of support from his relatives, Washington began "making life on the street." He started in the market.

"When we see a coal car come, we go unload it." The trucks arrived with flatbeds piled high above the side railings, lashed tight to keep the contents from brimming over the edge on the bumpy back roads and washed out urban byways. Young men tossed and carried huge sacks of the dusty black lumps of fuel, skittering through the congestion, nimble and agile in the sweaty flow of people and goods and traffic. "Then they give us small thing, you know? . . . It was very small. They give us 300 Liberian dollars

[LD].[1] Four persons, 300 dollars, so that money was not really enough to sustain me for the day."

When there was no day labor available, young men hustled for other opportunities. James related the way that he had worked to find his daily bread in the market: "Everybody sweep the market. Take the broom, and sweep the market. Okay, in the morning when the people come, we take plastic and we carry it around and say, 'oh, oh let me clean the table.' Yeah, that how we were doing things."

It was work done without request and in hopes of a small handout from the vendors. Busy intersections in the crowded parts of town were similarly inundated with young men hustling for small money. They called out and "fought" for cars on behalf of waiting bystanders. Whether requested to do so or not, they pushed their way through the clogged streets and sidewalks to find an empty seat, save it for a passenger, then ask and sometimes demand a fee of five Liberian dollars. Youth who hustled in such venues were literally fighting to push their way onto the goodwill of other people, hoping to be offered something in return for a service. There was no guarantee that passengers would give five LD for a saved seat. There was no certainty about the amount of small money that might be received for cleaning tables in the market. Making life in this way meant hard work in the present moment, done through uncertain conditions, with inconsistent returns on often frenetic and ongoing efforts.

Finding shelter was an equally crucial part of the hustle to make life on the street. One afternoon Joshua took me on a walking tour of the market area, pointing out dwelling after dwelling where he had been a temporary resident. "I used to live here . . . I used to live here." A dealer and a charming businessman, Joshua's customer base had grown to the point that he could be found wearing clean, button-down shirts, a thick roll of Liberian dollars folded into a bulging pocket. Before he had accrued the means to have a shelter of his own he had bounced all over the community, staying here and there to avoid sleeping on the street. All of his former shelters were in the households of friends or extended kin of some kind.

Joshua's patchwork of temporary living conditions was reflected in the circumstances of nearly all of the street youth I knew. It was dangerous to be caught out at night, alone and unprotected. The young men told stories of theft and abuse of people who were exposed in the late hours, vulnerable to violence and exploitation. Friends and family, unwilling to leave them out on the street at night, allowed some youth to stay beneath their roofs. James was staying with his sister in a mat hut in the backyard, Timothy with an elderly friend he called "uncle" out of respect, Washington with friends. Some were fed by those with whom they sheltered, others were not. Timothy could sleep at the elderly gentleman's house, but had to hustle for his own "daily bread."

Wanting to understand the extent of reciprocity that remained in their lives, I asked James and Washington about whether there were small boys and girls who were at least helping to wash their clothes or help in ways that younger household members typically served the older ones.

"You see . . . when you get a little brother, and you don't provide for them, they will not work for you," James explained.

"Yeah, they don't respect you if you don't have anything to give them," Washington chimed in.

"The first thing [you say to] a little brother," James continued, "'Come give me water, let me take bath.' But little brother will say, 'Every day I can bring you water what you do for me? What you have for me if I give you water?' It looks shameful [if you have nothing to give]. So we get up and we do our own thing by ourself."

Not only were youth in a delicate position with family members who provided for them without reciprocity, all were subject to varying degrees of stigma as unemployed, liminal young men who moved about the street. Tito, a timid member of the swath of young people in the area, related very shyly one day that he was allowed to sleep and eat at his sister's house, but that he was never trusted with money.

"They say I'm on the street. Her husband will not trust me. She will give money to her husband, but not to me."

"But what does that mean?" I probed. "You 'on the street?' You live with her. You eat [at] her house. What does that mean, you 'on the street?' You selling drugs?"

"Yeah."

There was a pervasive stigma associated with unoccupied young men smoking drugs in the street, and it led to feelings of abjection. Respectable parents and caregivers would not accept their sons choosing to deal or smoke drugs. "A real mother will not accept her child doing drugs," Timothy explained. "So you won't be with your parents and doing it." Liberians regarded smoking marijuana as dirty, degrading of one's character, and it was often accompanied, at least in the collective consciousness, with theft and other delinquent and problematic behaviors. The war was blamed. Flomo, who was quoted earlier, commented, "Some of our children, some of them they were vulnerable. During the war there were a lot of children who engaged themselves in war activities, child soldiers and other things. And within that, they began to take drugs. That not used to happen. Now, right now we're not fighting the war. But the remnant of the child soldier is still in our midst, polluting our children."

His use of the word "polluting" caught my attention. Others had spoken to me of the war as "spoiling" the children. "Polluting" offered a more vivid description. The remnant of the child soldier as a pollutant depicted a substance that had gotten into the young people, into the very tissues of society. Like a seeping toxin, the residue of "war activities" continued to ooze and contaminate. Goffman (1963) explains the experience of stigma as having been attributed with some natural quality that makes one "unfit." It denies the dignity enjoyed by onlookers and incurs their disdain. Stigma is at the root of many prejudices, attributing negative value to something innate in a person—the color of their skin or their sexuality, and in the case of these young men, appropriating delinquency with some kind of internalized drives left over from a time of pervasive violence and upheaval.

There is an important relationship between stigma and feelings of abjection, a relationship we ought not to miss. Abjection has been understood as an experience of social demotion (Ferguson 1999; Utas 2008), and this is an accurate use of the term. Jackson (2006, 43–44) pushes us deeper into the internalization of abject experience. It "can make a person feel as though he or she is a mere object," he writes, "nameless, of no count, ground down in a world where agency seems to be entirely in the hands of others." In this way abjection is more than being thrown down or demoted. For the street youth it was an experience of unworthiness, of being unfit based upon being young, male, and out of the house but not off of the street.

The contaminating effects of drugs translated to perceptions of youth who were seen as deviant, dangerous, and untrustworthy. We should also notice the conflation of stigma attributed to children and youth who fought in the war and engaged in "war activities," with all of the other youth.[2] Though Timothy had not participated with armed groups, in the public eye he was often cast as equally problematic to society, a burdensome result of the child soldier run amuck in his generation. "Anything, anything that happen, the people will say, 'Oh, it the youth again,'" Timothy lamented.

There was also a gendered demarcation to negative ascriptions applied to young people on the street. Young men were assumed to be stealing and engaging in "dirty" behavior such as smoking and selling marijuana. Girls were assumed to be selling their bodies, and many of them were.

"The girls, all in the street, selling theirselves for little bit of nothing," James commented. "Some of them can sell themselves for 50, 75 LD [for] fifteen minutes," which was roughly equivalent to one U.S. dollar at the time. While Liberians throughout my fieldwork spoke regretfully of the plight of young girls who were selling sex to survive, there was a different quality to their perception of young men. It was fearful and suspicious.

Though such stereotypes were oversimplified and often misapplied, there were many youth who earned the reputation that was applied to everyone. At one point Joshua mentioned to me, "You know you see those guys there," referring to an area near Timothy's place in Red Light. "They look common in the face but they do many things. They hijack. They pick pockets in the market when people are busy. For true." Some young people operated independently. They roamed through communities stealing batteries from parked cars, lightbulbs from porches, phones from preoccupied people in the market. Others became part of organized gangs. As far as I knew, none the young men I spent time with were actively working with gangs, though Timothy, Washington, and Joshua all alluded to former involvement with groups that stole and took advantage of other people.

Liberian adults regularly described this problem as a result of "peer pressure" and "bad friends." It sounded at times as oversimplified and pejorative as Singer's (2006) suggestion that children are so impressionable that they would participate in war on a mere whim. Timothy described something far more systemic:

> A teenager, yeah, around fifteen, sixteen, he start coming in the community, seeing people of his age playing with some kind of huge amount of money, 2,000, 3,000. He will go with them. At times they will share with him. . . . If you follow someone who is doing things for you all the time, it's like the person keeps helping you. And you don't have nothing. At the end of the day, you will be encouraged to follow the person. If the person is a rogue, one day he might initiate you, and you will become a rogue. They won't continue doing it for you all the time. So once you with them, at a certain point in time, you gotta pay. And you know you gotta do likewise for them too. So, they will force you, they will encourage you now to [start] stealing. That's how you [start] stealing. You're among your peer group. You are doing certain things that you know that—you don't like it at the time, but you want to maintain that relationship. And you know, for the maintenance of the relationship, you will be forced to do it.

When the helping hand was not there in families and extended kin, some young people found it in gangs. Incorporation into gangs has been described similarly in other contexts. One informant in Eugene Jarecki's (2012) film on drugs in the United States described the experience of being provided for by the drug lord in his neighborhood. Once a helping hand had been received, "it's like you were under him." There was an obligation created by receiving help from a patron, and reciprocity was required to "maintain the relationship."

In Red Light, I was not aware of any of the young men being actively involved with gangs. In fact, the ones who intimated former involvement with crime had brushed against experiences they were keen to avoid in the future. Timothy and Washington had done things they regretted, and had chosen to distance themselves from further violence or theft. Joshua got arrested and sent to jail.

"They took me into the Police Depot," Joshua related. "My mother came. She left me there. I spent three months in jail. She said it was better that I suffer and learn my lesson. So she didn't get me out. Since then, I have not done anything. I don't want to concern her."

Some time after his release he began selling marijuana. It was a means of survival in an urban terrain where there was not enough work, and gangs and crime presented stress that he wished to avoid. Being able to sustain himself meant that he was no longer a burden on others, or a worry to his mother, whom he wanted to please. Joshua is an example of a young man who was not thrown out or uncared for, but very much loved.

"One ex-general for Taylor . . . there's one big place where he can get it in the bush," Joshua said. "He brings it. Last time he brought it in big bags. I just buy a little bit to sell in our area. . . . You can make a little money. This Christmas I went up to see my mother in Buchanan. I took [a gift] and 500LD. She was pleased. She doesn't care if I sell the marijuana. She says she doesn't mind, as long as I'm providing for myself and staying out of trouble."

Though smoking and selling drugs was not a dignified way to make a living, selling drugs in the street enabled some youth to elevate their socioeconomic status above others. Cheap and addictive, marijuana and other drugs provided an ongoing, consistent means of small cash flow. Regular users meant that young men who sold marijuana could count on the cash flow in ways that youth who struggled for day labor could not. As "dirty" and deviant as it might be seen in public discourse, selling marijuana made it possible for Joshua to achieve social respect from his mother by becoming self-reliant, even able to provide for her in a small financial way. He achieved honor in her eyes. This pleased him, and it also meant that he dodged the feelings of abjection expressed by others.

Parenthood: Additional Dependents

Joshua was the most financially comfortable of any of the young men I knew in Red Light. He also had fewer outstanding obligations. One of the regular stressors in many of their lives was the added weight of parenthood without the material means to provide for children. Most of the youth I knew had "born" (produced) at least one child, and none of them were able to adequately fulfill their parental obligations.

"Early pregnancy is a problem," a woman explained in a focus group. "We tell them [young women] not to get pregnant. They become young parents. At the end of the day, your parents are struggling to support you—you get pregnant. The man can't support the child. He refuse the pregnancy. It brings the whole family down. We tell them to keep out of it. Unwanted pregnancies causing problem. The family is unable to maintain, the whole society is affected."

Young men felt the burden of their unfulfilled obligations quite acutely. I found James particularly fidgety on an afternoon I spent with him near his house just outside of the market.

"Your leg's been shaking since you sat down," I commented.

James explained that his ex-girlfriend would be coming to collect child support from him in the next few days. "I told her, I say, 'I not working. How will I afford that money?' The month coming to an end . . . the mother will come. If I don't get [the money together] the police will come."

"The police will come, and straight to jail if he does not pay child support," Washington piped in.

"It's very difficult. It's hard in life."

James's ex-girlfriend had been especially proactive. She had pressured him to provide for his young daughter, and when he couldn't, she had taken him to the police. At the station they had publicly reached an agreement about child support. If he could not fulfill that obligation, he feared she would come with the police to put him in jail for reneging on their contract.

Youth who were not attempting to satisfy the requests or demands for child support from the mother were often leaning on the willingness of others who, as Timothy's mother was doing, raised other people's children for them. Young men's inability to provide for and protect their children meant that they became indebted to others. Siblings, cousins, aunts, and uncles were called upon to foster children that young men were unable to manage. It was a position that was both shaming and stressful. Their networks of support were unable to assist them into independent adulthood, and in their prolonged youth, they created situations in which their insufficiency to parent their own children meant relying on the very people who were too overextended to help them in the first place. This is one of the ways that hierarchical webs of obligation became so bottom heavy. Dependents accrued far more rapidly than patrons who could care for them.

"Nothing Doing"

Life on the street, on the periphery of core networks of support, was inundated with all of these and other stressors—they were pervasive and continuous, mundane in the everyday. With no household to contribute to, no steady work or patron to answer to, most of the youth spent long hours watching the day go by. In the early weeks of fieldwork I wrote in my notes, "There are lots of youth you see sitting around, two or three to a little stand of oranges and Cokes—far more than are needed to sell them. There are often three or four sitting in the shade behind Stephen while he and his mates are selling scratch cards. They just sit and watch the day go by."[3] They reminded me of Mains's (2007, 659) observation of young men in Ethiopia, where there seemed to be little else to do than to watch the "contours of the shade from one side of the street to the other with the passing of the sun." "The day is reduced to little more than a mundane rhythm of slow, hot hours, spent smoking and sitting,"[4] I wrote later. "Haggling over who owes the other what thing or amount of money. They are not complaining. They are not striving. The boys there don't even seem to be waiting. They're just there. They're just living, existing. 'Nothing doing,' they say."

The haggling over which person owed someone what thing was a regular occurrence, and an important part of their reciprocity among one another. With no intergenerational patronage to rely on, they contributed to each other's survival in small ways.

"Darus! You can't pay my money?" Timothy called to someone one afternoon. I scanned the large, open passageway beneath the trees. It was well trafficked with petty traders moving in and out of the market area. "Darus where my trouser?" he continued. "I see used clothes." He continued to harass the young man who eventually came into view shouldering a large bag of used clothes. Darus smiled sheepishly and pulled a pair of jeans from the folded mass of clothing and handed them to Timothy.

"We use the barter system a lot here," Timothy noted, turning to explain the scenario to me. "Something for something. That's how we can do it. We share everything. If I don't have, maybe you do, and you will help me today. Tomorrow, maybe it will be me that has, and I will share with you."

Though youth were often sitting still, they were constantly on the watch for opportunities to make good on a debt or an opportunity to indebt themselves to someone who could help them. They were perpetually "scanning the environment" as Vigh (2012) recalled of the young men on the streets of Bissau. When Darus walked through the area by Timothy's place, Timothy began calling to him immediately, and did not let up until the young man acknowledged his debt and repaid it with a pair of jeans. Their circumstances offered few material comforts, and opportunities missed might not present again for quite some time.

Uncertainty has become a dominant trope in ethnographic work on the African continent. Cooper and Pratten (2015, 1) describe uncertainty as a lived experience in which a pervasive sense of vulnerability, anxiety, hope, and possibility compete for space in one's outlook. When socioeconomic resources are immensely depleted, and opportunities to better one's circumstances become consistently unpredictable, part of the tactic of everyday survival is to stay in a constant position of readiness to "pounce" (Hoffman 2011a) when chances reveal themselves.

One morning while we were smoking cigarettes I asked Timothy about a pastor who had been visiting him and his friends. He had come to offer spiritual encouragement in the past. Timothy said he had become busy, and no longer came out to their area in Red Light. Instead, he had told them to come by his house, where they could read the Bible and pray together. Timothy and the others refused.

"We can't just be leaving like that." There was indignation in his voice. "We have busy schedules, things to do. We can't just leave."

I looked around the area. Everyone was sedentary. The steady flow of petty traders continued, but none of the youth moved. There was "nothing doing."

"What would you miss if you left and went to see him?" I ventured carefully.

"Someone might come with something for me. How can I get it if I am not around?"

Indebtedness and obligation were only as good to young men as their access to those who owed them or could help them. They needed to be available and accessible and most did not have cell phones. Their remaining family, friends, or potential employers could not merely call up when opportunities arose. Those who did have phones often had no credit to make calls. It cost money to charge their phones at local stands like Stephen's. Those who possessed phones regularly switched them off to conserve battery life until they were needed to make a call. This meant that anyone who "had something" would have to find the person, or send a message to them through someone else.

Repayment of debts insured that one's social honor among peers was not diminished. The social honor, earned through reciprocity, strengthened trust and bolstered the durability of support among peers on the street. Social hierarchies of obligation and dependence emerged even in the small groups of youth at the margins of society. Young men like Timothy and Joshua rose high enough above their peers that their small amounts of cash and resources meant that others were often coming to them for help. However, the reciprocities that these young people maintained among one another could not provide the helping hand that was needed to get them out of the street and onto a viable pathway of socioeconomic achievement. It meant that most were trading favors and material goods among themselves. They were sustaining life on the periphery with little hope of transitioning off of the street and into more respectable trajectories toward adulthood.

Conclusion

The persistence of insidious ideologies like the New Barbarism or the loose molecules paradigm is due (at least partially) to the empirical evidence to which they are tethered. The urban capital was jammed with young men who had little to do. Some of them were aggressive at times, and involved in illicit activities for which their generation was stigmatized and bemoaned. As Philippe Bourgois (2003) reflected of the crack dealers in Harlem, with the structural limitations imposed on the entire country and especially in the densely crowded landscape of Monrovia, it was little wonder that youth with inhibited prospects and little support resorted to drugs. Unlike the depictions of street youth in the National Youth Policy, few of these Liberian young men were lost to caring adults, or entirely "turned loose." They were attached to one another and most remained attached to some form of kin relation, if not a close family member. The available support across generations had simply diminished to the point that young men were hustling on the street. The rejection of theft and violence that Timothy, Washington, and others exhibited demonstrates that they were far from the mindless reprobates they are so often portrayed as in local and international discourse. Those who sold drugs had become involved in dealing like Timothy and Joshua had—they were pressed to survive in an environment where other avenues were unavailable.

In many ways Stephen's life in the previous chapter is not much different from Timothy's. Both were no longer in the care of parents, or residing in their homes, and both were stressed by the difficulty of making life and finding their daily bread. The difference was that Timothy's livelihood incurred a stigma that Stephen's did not. Though both felt frustrated by the lack of opportunities in education and the economy, Stephen's money changing stand avoided the disrespect of the community, and the abjection that Timothy felt.

Joshua's relationship with his mother offers a thought-provoking example of how experiences of personal relationships can challenge and inform structural norms and values. Dealing drugs was the very sort of behavior that separated the dignified and respectable from the undignified and disrespected. It was the kind of thing that went along with being outside of the dominant group, and had no respectability in collectively internalized social norms. Joshua's mother takes exception, however, and regards him favorably for his self-reliance. Her assessment of him could be put down to the blind affection of a relieved mother, though for me it has prompted much reflection. It is an instance in which the terms of honor are adjusted. Joshua is providing for himself under extraordinarily depleted circumstances. He is as worthy of respect as honor in her eyes. Joshua was surrounded by peers who felt their abject social status acutely. By honoring his efforts, his mother seemed to defuse much of the weight of disdain levied by the dominant discourse. When I think about the buoyancy of his demeanor and his well-being among his peers, I am left with the sense that Joshua's mother has helped him claim a dignity not defined by the dominant, but rather bestowed in their relationships with one another as mother and son. If we understand the construct of dignity as a feeling of worth bestowed on individuals or collectives, then it is the value of the beholder that matters the most. If the gaze of his mother matters more than the evaluation of the dominant, then his dignity can be defined and claimed outside of "society's" regard for him. He is then released from the pressure to conform to a code of conduct that was not of his choosing any more than the socioeconomic status in which he was born and in which he struggled during the postwar recovery. His dignity could be the measure of his worth in her eyes and his honor could be earned under an adjusted code of conduct—one that respected his efforts as a dealer who was dealing with circumstances not of his choosing.

5
Life in Armed Groups

The violent social terrain in which young soldiers lost, formed, and renegotiated relationships of interdependence with armed groups is important to our understanding of reintegration. Their experiences of incorporation and fighting during the war are the subject of this chapter. It addresses the question of "why do they fight?" and presents my analysis of why that matters. Much of the literature has focused on vertical social transitions toward adulthood or status as big men. In this chapter, I argue that their horizontal transitions from families and communities to armed groups is just as vital to our analysis of their experience as their transitions from boys to men.[1]

Various theoretical and empirical accounts of youth involvement highlight certain aspects of conflict participation. I have approached my empirical material and the literature on young soldiers as though it were something of a knot, made up of many strands tangled together and bound up in youth experience. For example, rights-based approaches focus on victimization of young people while anthropologists tend to emphasize youth agency and resilience. Some research presents youth involvement in conflict as a time of increased life chances while others focus on abuse and trauma. The narratives of the young men in this chapter resonate with a number of discursive approaches to the topic. Rather than take aim at one or more of these theoretical strands, all of which have been brought to bear on a highly complex experience, the empirical material often holds competing theoretical interpretations in tension. I am comfortable with this, as I agree with Shepler (2014) that there is no single, overarching experience of "the war." The most important point to take away from this chapter is that participation with armed groups meant experiencing a significant rupture from core networks of support in families, kin, and communities. Young recruits became integrated into a new and alternative social context. The more nuanced and analytical our understanding of that experience, the more likely we are to grasp the challenges of "reintegrating" once the war was over.

I begin with the difficult story of Morris, an ex-combatant who served in Charles Taylor's Anti-Terrorist Unit. I have chosen to begin with Morris's account of becoming a soldier not to be shocking or sensational, but because his experience demonstrates the means by which armed groups had the power to terrorize civilians, how uncertain and violent the environment could be, and because his choice to fight with Taylor challenges some of the more basic and reductionist interpretations of why young people involve themselves with armed groups.

Morris's "War Story"

Morris was around the age of fifteen or sixteen when an armed group moved into his region and took over his village. He remembers walking into his community to find a shocking scene.

"They got a big town," he said. The rebels had moved through a bigger town on their way to where he was. "Yeah, and they catch all the people there. They catch the pastor. They kill the pastor, cut off the pastor' head. Put the pastor' head on a [stake] on the car road, so that anyone who come in the car road will see the pastor for the town that they killed. Killed the pastor son too. Kill him and put him by the pastor's side. Anybody come by that side will see the head.

"I was small at the time. I [was afraid]. Go straight in the bush. I pray. But after when I pray, I start creeping. Start creeping small, see the people digging the hole. I see them putting my people inside. . . . The rebel came, said 'we gonna put all of you together.' They dug a big hole. They put my little sister, my mother and my father inside . . . just waste dirt inside."

Morris watched from the bushes as everyone died, buried alive in a mass grave they had been forced to dig themselves.

"Not a small thing. I cry, shed tears . . . I run. I run hard. I take off my shirt, put it in my mouth for me not to shout."

He fled the village, running through the bush on his own, senses heightened for indications of rebel movement. He remembers running for three days. Eventually he came to a river crossing where there was a canoe. He got in and began to make his way across the water. Rebel soldiers spotted him crossing the river.

"The rebel see me, they start firing. That whole canoe, it was torn. During that time I was in water business . . . I swim, swim, swim. I was looking for the shore but I don't see the shore. . . . But there was a fisherman . . . I see the net. So I hang in his net, just like a fish, start crying, 'Hey! Somebody help me! Somebody help me!' Yeah, for that man to help me. The man carry me in the town. The man carry me in the town. He give me food to eat."

The fisherman quickly became a friend to Morris, a helping hand. He got him medicine. In the violent terrain in which his family had just been ruthlessly murdered, a friend and a supportive figure emerged to rescue him. When they felt it okay to move again, the man took him into the bush.

"During that time, we can't see war," Morris noted.

I would like to note that at many points during the research it was difficult to determine the time frames along which memories were strung together in the narratives of my informants. Each memory was also subject to the erosion and re-formation of events, feelings, and meanings, a metamorphosis that occurs over the passage of time, with the tricks of memory, and a past understood through a lens of the present (Schafer 2001). I am not sure how long their reprieve from the violence lasted in the town, or how long they were in the bush. However, it is painfully evident that it ended suddenly.

"The man got killed. They killed that man. Stray bullet kill him. We were not expecting it, nothing. It just bust his whole head. We were not expecting. He just die."

Morris could not cope with the insecurity and uncertainty of the violence any longer. He went straight to Charles Taylor's forces and volunteered to join. He referred to himself at that time as a "frustration child," an angry young man in Taylor's Anti-Terrorist Unit.

Motivations to Fight

Morris's experience leading up to joining Taylor's army illustrates two important themes common to most young men's stories. First, there was a degree of uncertainty and insecurity in the environment. One could never be sure when violence would occur or how it might manifest. Young people who joined would have the inside knowledge that might be helpful to their families, or so they hoped.

"The kids were keen about how they joined these guys [armed groups]," Peter remembered. An elderly gentleman, Peter's countenance was that of a man who had seen a great deal, and yet retained the spark and softness of a person who enjoyed life. He was involved in the rehabilitation and reintegration portion of the national DDRR process, and worked in a residential program with young ex-combatants who disarmed and demobilized. "They were keen in the sense that people were always asking them question. Many times they were asked that question, 'Why did you join these people?' They had their different stories. From angle to angle, they all had their stories about how they joined these guys. Some of their reasons were really life saving. They wanted to save their lives. Some of them would say 'when I got into the army I was able to rescue my family.' . . . So that why, you know, I'm stressin' how keen they were; because they felt that it helped them to save their families as well."

Humanitarian discourse about young fighters tends to coagulate around categories of recruitment such as "forced," "coerced," or "voluntary" (see Machel 2001; UN 2016b). The juxtaposition of "forced" recruitment next to "voluntary" can make it deceptively easy to slip into the notion that young people make decisions to join from within a vacuum, unprompted and of their own accord. Yet as Morris's experience demonstrates, in a habitus of war nearly everyone's daily lives were directly affected in some way by the presence of armed groups waging war in the country. No matter how much young people agreed with the "revolutionary" motivations pronounced by an armed group (Richards 1996), or believed that fighting might confer status that much of their generation lacked (Utas 2008), decisions to "volunteer" could not be made as "free choices." They were decisions taken in an environment charged with violence and exploitation that produced a pervasive sense of insecurity and uncertainty.

There are several dominant tropes regarding youth participation in armed conflict (see Murphy 2003). The rights-based discourse portrays young recruits as "coerced victims," forced into participation through abuse and manipulation by brutal abductors. A report from the war in Liberia refers to child soldiers in the title as "Easy Prey" (Human Rights Watch 1994). Some young people in this research were unwilling even to broach the subject of why they joined. Those who did share their experiences were usually abducted or intimidated, pressured into acquiescing to the demands of an armed group. Hurting family members was a common method of pushing them to join the ranks. This is a tactic that has been used in conflicts across the continent (see Marks 2013, 113), and it usually works.

"Yeah, because once you a soldier, nobody can embarrass[2] you," Boima explained. A former driver for Taylor's forces, he was articulate and reasoned about the constraints of the environment during the civil war. "They can't embarrass your family. But if you not a soldier, they will embarrass you and they will embarrass your family. They will continue to use you and your family. So you will look at that and say, 'No, I won't sit there and let this man who will know that I can do more than he to come and use me and my family.' So it would be better that I what? That I go and join to protect me and my family. So that what encourage more child soldier to go and join the revolution."

Scholars have challenged the rights-based discourse of youth as "easy prey," arguing that representations of children and youth who are "used" by others, without attention to their own decision making, political worldviews, or structural positions, denies their agency in the situation (see Boyden 2007; Hart 2008; Honwana 2005). The UN (2016b) takes the position that the distinction between voluntary and forced recruitment is *meaningless*, because all participation is the result of a desperate attempt to survive. This appears overreaching. I would argue that while no one of any age makes a "free choice" to fight in wars (see Rosen 2007), there are certainly degrees of agency applied by actors who take up arms. The response to the rights-based approach builds from a body of work in the critical sociology of childhood, in which theorists challenge the discourse on the "rights of a child" in developing countries as a misappropriation of Western norms and values about childhood as a time of innocence and immaturity (see James and Prout 1990). They argue that such representations lead to constructions of children and young people as passive receptacles for input from adults and society. Within the context of armed conflict, Hart (2008) insists that children are acutely aware of their sociopolitical circumstances, that they exercise their own agency within war zones, and that they are much more than mere victims of circumstance or coercion.

I am inclined to agree with Jeffrey (2012) that we are now well accustomed to the notion that young people "have agency." It is the extent to which they are able to exercise choice, and to take action, that interests me in this work. Morris's experience of losing his family, running from the soldiers, and eventually joining Taylor's forces demonstrates how constrained any sense of control could become in a habitus of war. Most of the young men in this study were acting from positions of very limited agentive capacity. Their options were few, and the implications of their choices were enormous, often fatal. It seems more helpful to me to think about coercive methods and forced recruitment in terms of power *to* versus power *over*. These young men were faced with armed groups who had power over them. They came in uninvited and held the means to life and death. Youth had power to choose fates that were *imposed* upon them. If they joined they believed that they would no longer be in a position where their lives could be placed in these dominated positions. Joining a group and holding a gun would give them both power to act in a less constrained scope of possibilities and power over others through their possession of weaponry and their incorporation with a mobilized group.

In Sierra Leone, Richards (1996) has argued that young people fought consciously, out of convictions that the dominant political regime had restricted their life chances. This echoes Hart's (2008) assertions earlier. In Liberia, though some ex-combatants occasionally referred to "the revolution," and to fighting in order to make things better in the country, there is no evidence of any substantial, ideological foundation that guided the politics of warring factions, not least of which was the National Patriotic Front of Liberia, which was responsible for the inception of war.

Even in Sierra Leone, where the use of the Muammar Gaddafi's political philosophy espoused in the Green Book was incorporated into the rhetoric of the military campaign of the Revolutionary United Front, scholars have held serious objections to Richard's assertions that youth conscientiously participated for political reasons.[3] The included authors insist that Richards overstepped his ability to understand the context for war in Sierra Leone. They portray youth as relatively delinquent, and Richards as attempting to apply logic and reason to what was, in Abdullah's (1997) frank assessment, senseless and irrational violence. There are certainly reports of marginalized youth from the streets who took the opportunity to fight with armed groups in wars like those in Sierra Leone and Liberia (Cohn and Goodwin-Gill 1994; Zack-Williams 2001). There is no doubt that some marginalized youth found a support system and a purpose in armed groups. It seems quite likely that they were easy to recruit, though we should be careful not to extrapolate this idea of "delinquent youth" as alienated opportunists. Most of the ex-combatants in this research were not on the street waiting for something better to do. They were not "idle" and vulnerable to conscription by promises of material wealth or increased social status. They were like Morris. They lived with families and within communities. They were pressed to join out of fear for their lives and those of the ones they loved. This pattern of joining is reflected in more representative, and quantitative, data with ex-combatants in Liberia (see Pugel 2007), which finds that the majority of recruits joined out of fear or as a means to protect loved ones.

All of this said, I assert that the distinction between voluntary and forced recruitment is *absolutely meaningful.* All agents operate within structural parameters, the vast majority of which are not under their direct control. Their choices and their actions within those boundaries have much to tell us about power and possibility. There is a significant difference between Boima's description of choosing to fight to preserve the family from embarrassment, and having the opportunity to choose that path taken away by a soldier at the tip of a gun barrel or the edge of a machete. In the first instance, a decision is made and acted on, and there is ownership of a choice. In the latter there is helplessness. They are not the same. Though the degree of choice between these two examples may appear small, even minute, in such violently charged arenas, to conflate one with the other is to suggest that all young people are mere victims of circumstance, that adults (persons eighteen years of age and older) are not, and that only the decisions of adults are of consequence. In fact, many young people around the world take risks and make decisions that have enormous impacts on their lives and those of others. Surely their action under such immense pressure is worthy of a meaningful distinction between voluntary enlistment and absolute, victimizing force.

Initiation and Inoculation

Armed groups became the relational and institutional supports that in many ways replaced families, kin, and communities. This is not to say that young people were always cut off from families. However, it is evident that their incorporation into armed groups required that they realign their allegiance to hierarchical networks of comrades and commanders. Much has been written and speculated about the rituals and training practices that are used to turn young people into soldiers, especially those practices that have spiritual and secret elements to them. While media coverage of wars like those in Liberia and Sierra Leone put the exotic and bizarre on display, anthropologists have responded with interpretations that are primarily concerned with grounding initiations in context. They inquire and make arguments about the extent to which initiation practices are new, or renewed from long-standing cultural processes and beliefs, and seek to interpret what they really mean or symbolize. In the following discussion, I have tried to offer a thoughtful contribution to this literature from the narratives of the ex-combatants in my work. What is apparent to me is that there is a great deal that we simply cannot know about rites of passage in war. What we can be sure of is that they signal transitions into a violent community, and a violent way of life.

Becoming a member of an armed group meant entering a new social entity. Young soldiers were trained through boot camps in some instances, and apprenticeship under comrades in others. My data cannot support a substantive analysis of training practices, as I spoke with ex-combatants from a number of factions who had participated at different points in the war. The extent to which there was a training regime commonly used among factions is unclear. Certainly, rebel groups have used training protocols that reflect much more order than the rag-tag stereotype that has been applied to armed groups in Africa (see Marks 2013). Some of my informants who joined early in the 1990s recalled boot-camp-like experiences that varied in detail, while others who joined later remembered much more informal mentorship under seasoned fighters.

Much of the interest in initiation, rites of passage, and preparation to fight has been concerned with social transitions within West African civil wars. For instance, Ellis (2003, 2) suggests that forms of initiation into armed groups resemble traditional initiation rituals "used to manage transformation of children into adults." I am cautious about this assertion on two counts. I am cautious of what has become a relatively standard "boys to men" narrative that links youth initiation with a rather instantaneous transformation to "adulthood." I am also cautious concerning inferences made about how ritual practice was locally understood in the context of armed groups.

Moran (2006) jabs at anthropologists for their "obsession" with secret hierarchies in West Africa, where secret societies and their occult practices have been a source of deep intrigue for scholars. She believes that the focus on secret rituals has distracted theorists from other interpretations that are pertinent to an understanding of the structural environment. The fascination is understandable. "Bush schools" in Poro secret societies (hierarchical leadership councils within and across ethnic groups throughout West Africa), are rich with exhibitions of high drama, intrigue, and identity exploration. The sensational displays of costume, kidnapping, and training recounted by ethnographers like Bellman (1984) are unquestionably exciting. During bush school, Poro elders were given complete oversight of youth. Young men were kidnapped by their elders and taken into the bush behind an enclosed space. They were symbolically "eaten" by a spirit in the forest and given cuts that would scar, marking them as members of the Poro. They were not allowed to leave, nor was there any visitation by their families. When they were returned, they had been taught how to survive in the bush, to hunt and fish. They were taught the secrets of the Poro tradition and a devout respect for the community of elders. This was an education that took two to three years in the bush, if not longer in the days before modernization crept into rural communities and infused its social and political structures with a value for formal (Western) schooling (Little 1965). When young men were returned to their communities and their families they had been given a new name. They were to be treated differently by their mothers. They were no longer "small boys."[4]

There are clear similarities between some of the primary rituals used to prepare youth for life in rural society and those used by rebel groups like the Revolutionary United Front in Sierra Leone and the NPFL in Liberia (Ellis 2003; Richards 1996, Shepler 2005, 2014). Young men were commonly abducted and taken into the bush. They were cut to create scars marking them as members of their units. They were given medicines to inoculate them from enemy fire, and trained to fight and to respect the social hierarchies of the group. If there is a tendency toward fascination with bush school in its original form, it certainly has not lost its cultural interest once armed rebel movements adopt aspects of those ritual practices. The emphasis on rituals that "transform" youth into adults places the majority of attention on the ritual itself, and on rituals as spiritual practices that move young people from one social category to another (see Bragg 2006; Ellis 2003). The extent to which these ceremonial elements of initiation transitioned them from young boys or "youth" into adults seems an exercise in speculation. It is possible that young people felt themselves given a new charge, a purpose, and a responsibility that reflected a more mature social status. Yet initiation practices and trainings in armed groups did not last for nearly the length of time that traditional bush schools had. My informants remembered time scales that varied from a few weeks to a few months. This seems to have been dictated at least in part by the manpower needs of the armed group, and the manpower availability to formally train new recruits as the war progressed. My conversations with young men indicated that higher social status as adults and even as "big men" was achieved through performance as soldiers, and acquired over time. They came to feel "big" through executing orders, running missions, and achieving recognition for victories and successes that were important within the context of their military unit. In short, achieving higher social status occurred more through performance and experience over time than through ritual and symbolic initiation.

One of the most prolific parts of the initiation and preparation of new recruits was a bulletproofing ritual, which was practiced by most factions, and has been observed throughout West Africa (see Hamer 2011; Hoffman 2011b; Marks 2013). A young man named Sekou remembered his bulletproofing experience with the NPFL as follows:

> They force you to go to the medicine man. They do different, different things to you. It is to help make you to be brave. . . . The medicine man marks you, he gives you medicine. You have to take the medicine. Then they stand you up against a palm tree. You know Arnold? You see Terminator? They stand you up. They fire automatic weapons at you [he motioned to indicate big guns like AK-47s]. It's just like Arnold. The bullets do not penetrate. It feels like someone is chunking small rocks at you, or like rain hitting you. The bullets cannot hurt you. It makes you brave."

In his detailed and attentive account of bulletproofing among the Kamajor fighters in Sierra Leone, Hoffman (2011b) describes bulletproofing practices as military innovations, as new spiritual protections designed in response to modern weaponry wielded during the civil war. Though the actual rituals and medicines themselves may have been new recipes and practices created to protect the Kamajors in their current situation, the actual act of spiritually imbuing fighters with invincibility is not a new innovation within the region at all. In Liberia, there is a long tradition of using medicine for protection during warfare. Individual warriors could have medicine prepared by a Zo (also known as a medicine man) in the form of various objects such as skins, teeth, beaks, and so forth, to ward off blows, to cause invisibility and invincibility to arrows and gunfire (Schwab 1947). It is an old ritual practice applied to current warfare where modern, automatic weapons would test its strength.

Analytical attendance to a site of new innovation or continuity of tradition is important. It demonstrates a critical and careful treatment of another culture, one that avoids the pitfalls of exoticizing narratives to which this region is no stranger. In our attempts to accurately situate what is "new" or "old," which phenomena presents a break with norms or a pattern continued, it is also important that we do not miss the functionality of these events in our quest to understand the symbolism and cultural relevance. Young men, and more than a few young women, were being equipped to handle new responsibilities, ones that could be quite deadly. The act of bulletproofing was described by soldiers and their initiators as a ceremony of high drama. As Sekou related, young men were literally fired upon in front of their comrades as a demonstration of the power of their newly applied protection. This ceremony also signified a dramatic transition into a violent life, one that was quite removed in most respects from the lives they had lived in their home communities and with their families.

Fighters used other forms of medicines and drugs in addition to bulletproofing. "Medicine" as it was commonly used referred to conjured spiritual powers that were housed in objects that could be worn, or in substances used to provide protections of specific kinds.[5] Sekou had a valuable ring that he wore when he was a general for the NPFL. The ring warned him when danger was coming. He explained how it would begin to hurt his finger, signaling the approach of something bad. If food was offered to him under these circumstances he knew to abstain, as it might be laced with poison. If it was hurting him while with his men, he knew it was time to pack up, and he would order them to break camp and leave. A variety of charms, rings, and necklaces made of teeth or other materials were worn or carried by soldiers to protect them from harm.

If medicine could prepare soldiers to face the guns, drugs helped to empower them to use guns of their own. Drugs were a powerful source of mental separation from conscience and emotion.

"Anybody can understand why they did what they did," Michael observed of his ex-combatant peers. "In order to numb their fear, in order to do what they did, you get what I'm saying? The humiliation—they must take something to remove that sense of normalcy, that sense of consciousness."

Substance use among soldiers enabled them to distance themselves from the emotional response that would ordinarily occur in strenuous and violent situations where their lives could be taken from them and where they were under orders to take the lives of others. Because drugs chemically modify a sense of reality, the lived experience of fighting was literally changed, and became a less emotional or familiar human experience.

Thomas, a former NPFL soldier, had access to cocaine during the war. "When I was given gun, I take drugs. I take cocaine . . . real cocaine, that if I see you, I see you like an animal. I shoot you good. I kill you, and I don't think, because I was in drug . . . I was addicted to drugs. If I don't take drug, I won't eat, I won't do anything. [They] give it to the child soldiers to make the brain brave for us to do things."

Rampant use of hard drugs like cocaine is a staple component of the human-rights-based objections to youth participation in war (Coalition to Stop the Use of Child Soldiers 2008; Human Rights Watch 2004). Though there are former fighters like Thomas who recall being given drugs by commanders, the extent to which this was formal military procedure is not clear. Some of the ex-combatants in my work remembered using cocaine, which they obtained through commanders, others remember smoking marijuana, but were not exposed to cocaine, opiates, or other stronger substances.

"We had marijuana, or grass," Michael remembered. "There was a big place in Bong County. The grass came from there. There was cocaine, but I didn't see much of that. In my experience, only the big generals really had that. Most of the soldiers didn't really see much of it. We had the grass and the cane juice, Talent White, sleeping pills. It would make you to feel drunk. Yeah, real drunk. You take five or ten of those and you feel real drunk. It makes a sort of white saliva around your mouth. Soldiers would be talking real slowly."

"What was the purpose of wanting to feel drunk like that?"

"It changes the way you see things. If you see a man he will be looking real short, like a small person. He will be looking like an animal, short, you will not be afraid. You don't feel pain. You're not afraid."

"What do you mean you don't feel pain? You don't feel pain inflicted upon you, or the pain of inflicting harm on someone else?"

"Both. You won't feel it as much if you get hurt because of the drugs. But you won't feel that pain in harming someone else, either. . . . A lot of it too, was to make you look fearful. The drugs would turn your eyes red. People would be afraid when they saw you. There was also a leaf that they would take and squeeze the juice in their eyes. It made them turn red. This was all to make us look fearful."

It is possible that warlords at the highest levels of authority sanctioned or provided hard drugs such as cocaine, or both, though there is no concrete evidence (as far as I am aware) that warlords like Charles Taylor or Prince Johnson administered these drugs to their troops. This is an important point to raise because it calls the human rights discourse into question. The argument from rights groups is that children were coerced and forced to take addictive substances. Many were drug dependent, though not all, and the extent to which drug use was forced under the duress of abusive commanders is unclear. Most soldiers recalled drugs as merely part of the practice of preparing for combat, as fixtures of the environment more than substances taken under orders or due to addiction.

"Spiritual" medicine and drugs were two of the most highlighted aspects of soldier life that were highlighted in memories shared by the ex-combatants and noncombatants in this study. These substances signified a drastic difference between the soldiers' experience of the war, and the wartime experiences of others. Young men were participating in a violent way of life, one that was supported by supernatural protection as well as some drug-induced mental and emotional distance from foes and victims. They were usually cited as a primary indicator of the vast difference between life as a small boy in a town or village, and life as a young fighter in an armed group.

Becoming Men

There is now an established body of work identifying young people's feelings of prestige during war and the young men in this chapter add to that observation. In this section and the next, I highlight the social relations that were built during the war, and reflect on how these new hierarchical relations were woven over time through reciprocity and how they had important implications for respect. Relationships forged during the conflict are also vital to the analysis presented in the next chapter about ex-combatant reintegration.

There is widespread observation of affectionate relationships of exchange between commanders and their recruits, though some assert that these are still the product of manipulation and coercion (see Boothby, Crawford, and Halperin 2006; Schafer 2004). It is impossible to know how abusive or intimate such relations were without firsthand empirical data. Ex-combatants remembered different experiences of abuse and affection, and the variance is undoubtedly due to particular social and structural relations that were specific to their different units. Morris recounted an incidence of violence dealt to a small boy who disobeyed an order from their commanding officer. His story conveys a tremendous exercise of brutality, similar to violent discipline and abuse that has been reported throughout wars across the continent (see Cheney 2005; Honwana 2005; Machel 2001).

"The general gave us an order to kill our friend."

"I said 'I will not do that.' The general beat me."

"He beat you?"

"Yeah."

"He beat you for not killing your friend?"

"Yeah, because I was [looking out] for my little friend. I was too wicked. If anybody will do bad I will kill you. But I decide [not to do it, not to kill my friend]. So they beat me and all. Then the general end up killing the man." Morris's superior beat him, and ended up killing his little friend, though in the end, despite his threats, he spared Morris.

I cannot speak to the extent to which coercion occurred in the ranks or how brutal and violent the chain of command could become. However, it was evident that brutality and aggression were not the only or even the most defining features of hierarchical relationships in armed groups. Randall, who drove a truck for the NPFL during the war, spoke confidently and affectionately of his relationship with his former commander.

"We been together during the crisis," he remembered. "During the crisis we were friends. He can't leave me. When I in problem, he in problem. So he was more like a brother. We were all together. We move like that, like a brother. Yeah, that how we live together . . . serving each other' life. . . . [It was] the same man (commanding officer) that been with every one of us. . . . He brought us up during the crisis. We work for him. He like a godfather for us. That the man that take care of us, do everything for us."

Armed groups were a new social platform in which young people's life chances continued to be supported through interdependent and intergenerational relationships. From his work in Sierra Leone, Hoffman (2011b, 133) relates:

> As a patron, a "commander" would be responsible for his "clients" in ways not defined by military necessity or protocol. In addition to providing food, shelter, weapons and ammunition, a patron-commander would be a resource in family emergencies or an arbiter for disputes among equals. He would be expected to stand for those beneath him in cases where allegations were made by local authorities or others within the movement. In return, the patron-commander's dependents would be expected to offer security for the "big man," share a portion of whatever wealth they might accumulate, and tend to his needs as necessary.

Participation with armed groups meant establishing new wealth in people. Survival, security, and status were embedded in relationships within the ranks. That is not to say that no one had patronage with families or kin outside of armed groups. However, their loyalty and allegiance was to armed groups first, and it was within that social order that some young men developed relationships that would sustain their lives and increase their status.

The gun gave young people the capacity to control others like they had never done before. Recalling his training with the NPFL, Michael explained, "They would say to us, 'the gun is your mama and your papa.' It meant that the gun could give you everything you need. If you have the gun, it can give you the money you need, the power you need, the car you need."

Guns gave young men positions of dominance. They did not have to ask parents to buy them things. They could take them from unarmed civilians, or scavenge through the spoils of a new territory.

"A soldier man have authority," David recalled. "He violate at any time against the civilian. You understand? He do his will at any time. A soldier man can choose, because he with gun. You know, what he want [he get] because he got gun against the civilian, so that he got authority. Civilian are much afraid."

Podder (2011) argues that the gerontocratic and patrimonial nature of Liberian society underwent a reversal during the war. She notes that "violence and symbolic power of the gun became a source of power and authority over parents and elders, often at the behest of obedience, compliance and respect which for generations had been inculcated into youth to perpetuate a gerontocratic hierarchy" (59). This was true to the experience of many encounters between civilians and combatants. Armed with weapons and the support of a military force, very young boys were allowed to demand material goods and services from very elderly unarmed civilians who were no longer in positions of authority over them, to whom their allegiance was no longer attached.

During a focus group in West Point, an elderly gentleman named Elijah remembered encountering young fighters. "I walk by small child, like my grandchild, holding arm [gun]. They killed fifty-seven people. But the day before they killed sixty people. They 'pop-pop-pop-pop'!," he related, making the sound of gunfire, his eyes wide. "'Papé, you will move!,'" he remembered being ordered.

Rather than a total reversal of gerontocratic norms, young fighters experienced a more fundamental break with social life outside of their factions. Age hierarchies appear to have persisted within the ranks. Taylor's forces were known for having "small boy" units. Young ones were put in their own unit, with their own set of military responsibilities, much like children were set apart for particular household tasks within the home. Prior to the war, young people would not have been able to speak to Elijah as they do in the above quote. With their guns and with their position in an armed faction, young men were given dominance over unarmed elders. In short, there was a sharper break with society outside of armed groups, rather than a universal inversion of gerontocracy.

Earlier I argued that while it is difficult to know how much status was conferred through ritual initiation, it is evident that young people achieved benchmarks of social status through performance of roles and responsibilities (see Utas 2003). Armed groups offered a helping hand that accelerated socioeconomic mobility during the war. At a very basic level, being part of a faction meant that the daily necessities of life as well as additional material possessions were readily available. Rations like rice, cassava, and liquor were provided on a regular basis.

"As a soldier I eat on time," Nathaniel commented.

It was a stark contrast to his postwar situation and that of many of his friends. But as a soldier in the NPFL his needs had been taken care of. In addition to basic provisions, anything that could be taken from civilians or from the front lines as spoils of war would add to a soldier's wealth.

"Some people love the operation," Michael reflected, "where they go on attack. When you go on attack, and your enemy retreat, whatsoever in that environment comes to you: looted materials, arms, you know whatsoever, water, soap, rice, yeah the drinks."[6]

"Because of looting properties," Peter explained, "looting cash, they [young fighters] began to establish families. They began to live on their own, earn money during the war by using gun during the war to earn money. They began to behave like men. They began to behave like a man and take responsibilities."

Fighting with armed groups enabled sustainable livelihoods and prospects for starting families, or at least maintaining relationships with girlfriends (see Coulter 2009; Utas 2005b). Young people were able to instruct and demand goods and services from civilians because they were armed. Within the ranks, as new recruits became more seasoned they were given responsibilities over others. All of these markers of greater socioeconomic maturity were associated with adulthood—and all of them were earned over time, and through experience and performance of roles and responsibilities.

Becoming Big Men

Recall how the street youth described big men in chapter 3. They ride in cars. They have houses and other people work for them. They hold positions, most of them in the government. And when they come into the community, they want to be popular, and they help people. Some of the ex-combatants in this work were able to take on responsibilities and to act not just in ways that reflected adulthood but that earned them status as bigger men. None of my informants were among the top generals who collaborated with warlords like Charles Taylor, Roosevelt Johnson, or Ahlaji Kromah. However, some of them were given responsibilities that reflected status as bigger men. Sekou's experience with the NPFL is a case in point.

Sekou was recruited during the earliest months of what became a very long war. When he was twelve or thirteen, he was taken from his school in Nimba County to be initiated and trained to fight with the NPFL. He rose through the ranks and told me stories of operations he led. Once, Charles Taylor personally thanked him for a successful operation he executed to capture a town in a strategic area. Taylor gave him cash money as a reward for himself and his men. We talked about his role as a leader and his reputation for being impartial—he would punish even his friends if they stepped out of line.

"What do you miss about being a soldier?," I asked.

Commanding his men, came the immediate reply. "Telling this one to go there, telling this one to go there," he motioned.

"You miss being in charge?"

He smiled, and I wondered if I had embarrassed him. "Yeah. Sometimes when we were camped, we get food, and we make it for all the town people. We have musicians come in to entertain us. We'd have enough liquor, beer. Everyone would come. It would be a time of enjoyment. I really miss that."

"You liked treating people?"

"Yes. It was a part of my job. I would take care of the people."

He was a general, commanding hundreds of men at points—a significant number of dependents who looked up to him. It was a position that afforded him the prestige that came through victory, and through dominance and displays of largesse. He could prominently and proudly bestow gifts and services on his men and on civilian communities they occupied—garnering greater honor and prestige all along the way.

For a young man not yet in his thirties at that time, this was an inconceivable position to be in outside of the context of the war, both in regards to generation and to class. Big men who had positions in dense networks of wealth in people were well past their early twenties. Most were also strongly attached to the government, and deeply indebted among the ruling class of Americo elites prior to Samuel Doe's takeover of state power. Young men in rural villages and towns were unlikely to gain the sort of power and prominence of big man status to begin with, and especially at such young ages.

Conclusion

There is much we cannot know about the complexity of the interpersonal and social experiences of becoming young soldiers. The child soldier phenomenon is well trod with speculation and with accounts that emphasize the sensational and extreme aspects of being young and being soldiers. Such accounts often downplay other structural forces that are enormously important for our understanding of conflict participation and postwar experience. There were two transitions during wartime that provided an essential foundation for ex-combatant's life chances after war. One was a horizontal transition to a new, hierarchical network of support in armed groups. The primary labor and allegiance of young people shifted from families, kin, and communities to comrades and commanders. They were under new patrons, and became patrons to others in a social system that was supported by engagement in warfare. The other was a vertical transition into higher socioeconomic status on an individual level.

Higher social status achieved over time became a point of interpersonal tension for many in the aftermath of the war. Young men invested years of their lives, their energy, their bodies, and their intellect with armed organizations that recognized their achievements and rewarded their efforts. Noncombatants, most of whom were deeply affected by the violence and exploitation these young soldiers exercised, were unable to appreciate their achievements as soldiers. Those achievements came at the immense, unquantifiable cost of lives, injuries, rape, and destruction of property and livelihoods. Many ex-combatants felt themselves at odds with those who could not recognize their bigger status, achieved through intense and demanding experiences of participation with armed groups. I say this not to sympathize with the aggression and dominance practiced by armed groups but to highlight how the intense experiences of fighters over time could mean a great deal during the war, but lose efficacy when ex-combatants transitioned to social situations beyond the ranks. Their negotiation of these and many other postwar social dynamics are discussed in the following chapter.

6

Life after Guns

Reintegration as Social Process

In postwar contexts ex-combatants are the subjects of numerous reactions and stereotypes that are more often than not marked with alarm and panic (Boyden 2007; Denov 2012). Much of the policy discourse, and a good deal of academic rhetoric, presents ex-combatants and former child soldiers in binary terms. They are victims or perpetrators. Rights-based and psychological literature advocate help for the victims, while postwar policy discourse highlights the necessity of managing ex-combatants through security measures designed to prevent them from ruining fragile peace agreements. At each end of these polarized perspectives, ex-combatants are objectified as entities that must be dealt with in particular ways. By extension, reintegration becomes a set of measures to be implemented or achieved. One of my primary aims at the outset of this research was to probe past these objectifications of former fighters. This chapter builds from a body of anthropological work previously conducted with former soldiers in West Africa (see Shepler 2014; Utas 2003; Vigh 2006a). It describes and explains the experience of reintegration as an ongoing, fluid process in which ex-combatants relate and act along a continuum of experience that is not captured in much of the literature. All of the contributors to this chapter had been victims and perpetrators of violence. A good deal of their postwar transitions out of armed groups were spent managing social stigma associated with them as violent killers, and with a quest to reassert or establish honor and prestige in the absence of the armed organizations that provided the ways and means to achieve respect during the war. This chapter builds on the previous empirical chapters, demonstrating that reintegration is a relational process. Thus far we have seen that survival, honor, and prestige are achieved in networks of social relationships. The same is true for ex-combatants. Their processes of reintegration were defined by those among whom they were interdependent and with whom they sought to achieve honor and prestige once their armed groups were no longer waging war.

Much of the content in this chapter is drawn from time I spent in Slipway, sitting and talking with the young men there in the same way that I spent time sitting and talking with the youth in chapter 4. Slipway is a small community tucked beneath the bypass to Capitol Hill and right next to the waterway leading to the ocean. In the mornings men clustered in the shade around the public toilets. They sat on stones or stairs, propped themselves against the chain-link fence, cigarettes hanging loosely between their rough dark brown fingers. We spoke about politics, the state of the country, and I asked for time to speak with them individually as I did with Timothy and the youth in Red Light. I did interviews with ex-combatants in Gardnersville and Bernard's Farm as well. However, these areas were further afield, and so the greater bulk of my time with ex-combatants was spent in Slipway, talking and passing the time outside of the public toilets.

Making Life outside of Armed Groups

Titus, a student at the University of Liberia, commented about his peers, saying:

> When the war ended, people were confused. . . . What made them confused was because they were used to one person who had authority. That was Charles Taylor. Then Charles Taylor left . . . So you know, most youth, you know most of them were fighters. After the war, the person who gave them the authority

> was no more. So you could just find young people roaming the street not doing anything, not having any sense of direction.

His observation provides a useful starting point for the overarching theme of this chapter. In the previous chapter we observed young men being culled out of their families and communities and embedded within a new web of hierarchies that organized their everyday lives, gave them purpose, and guided their social and economic transitions. They were taken from one set of relational systems and placed into another. Transitions out of armed groups were confusing for many because these transitions lacked the clarity and purpose that transition *into* armed groups had. Going into armed groups, young men quickly learned what was expected, what their role was, and to whom they must answer. Coming out of armed groups was very much the opposite. There was almost a sense of being dumped out of armed groups and into an ambiguous postwar social terrain.

That is not to say that there was no structure to their transitions. The final ceasefire occurred in June 2003. The Comprehensive Peace Agreement was signed in August2003. Charles Taylor accepted asylum in Nigeria, and by December 2003 the United Nations–supported disarmament and demobilization of armed groups was under way in Monrovia. Disarmament and demobilization continued in other parts of the country later in 2004. Ex-combatants who participated received 150 U.S. dollars for their weapon. Most were taken to cantonment sites where they spent five days undergoing "psychosocial support" activities (see NCDDRR 2006). Ex-combatants recalled being told not to take drugs and how to live in "normal" society. They were issued ID cards that they could use to identify themselves at vocational and educational programs set up specifically for them. If training was completed, another 150 U.S. dollars was given to enable them to start businesses of their own. Young people under the age of eighteen were taken to Interim Care Centres where they received counseling and some education, ranging between a few days up to three months.

By their own admission, the United Nations Mission in Liberia and the Joint Implementation Unit were unprepared to conduct a thorough DDRR process. The primary emphasis was placed upon disarmament and demobilization. "Rehabilitation" and "reintegration" were never properly defined, prioritized, or implemented in an effective way (NCDDRR 2006). This research demonstrates that part of that ineffectiveness lies in the manner in which reintegration was understood—as a process by which ex-combatants gained civilian status and the means to earn a sustainable living. It was conceived of as a project to put ex-combatants "back" into society (McMullin 2013). This institutional objective to put ex-combatants "back" leads McMullin to ask "back into what?"

When their armed groups were disbanded and, with them, their way of making life, these social and material foundations were replaced with promises of skills training and livelihoods through DDRR. However, for most of the young men in this research, these promises came to little fruition in an economically strapped postwar job market.

"If you come and take the gun from my hand, and just send me, to whom are you sending me to?," Sumo queried. A former general for the NPFL, he was pointed about the social repercussions of his conflict participation. "To my father who I have abused and disrespected because the power of the gun I was carrying? To whom are you sending me to?"

One of the most salient limitations of promoting reintegration through skills training lies in the lack of opportunities in an economically depleted context. Where opportunities do exist, they are embedded in social networks of trust and respect. The international agenda to put ex-combatants "back" falls flat for former fighters who have no one to go "back" to. Because life chances are so deeply embedded in reciprocal and hierarchical social relations, "back to *whom*?" was the primary question that ex-combatants had to answer.

So many young people lost their families to death and displacement during the war. For others, families were alive and living in the country, but unwilling to receive them. David recounted a recurring theme of social isolation among ex-combatants after the war. I saw him often in Slipway. He wore a soft expression, worn clothes, and when there was no day labor, he could be found lazing about, smoking or drinking cane juice, "nothing doing." A former soldier with Taylor's forces, he had been abducted to fight before completing high school. When the war ended he was twenty years old.

"No job," he related. "Because of the war, you know. Because after war business, people take me to be a bad guy. . . . People say I'm a rebel, you know. All kind of stuff. [I wound up] on the street, making my own way through, yeah. . . . I cannot go home. They will not take me. . . . So I call to talk to them [parents], make them understand, and they just left myself on the street."

Like Timothy, he eventually made a friend, someone who was willing to let him sleep in his room while he hustled for his daily bread. It is possible that some ex-combatants were rejected out of preservation of family honor—a sense of shame that their children were involved in committing the atrocities of war. Detailed research with the families of ex-combatants was beyond the scope of this work, and without adequate data, it is best not to speculate about what motivated family rejection of former fighters. What was apparent to the informants of this work, both ex-combatants and noncombatants, were ascriptions of deviance and dangerous behaviors that made former fighters untrustworthy and instilled fear in other people.

Recall the elder Flomo's description of the remnant of the child soldier as a pollutant. There was a pervasive perception of former soldiers as having been altered by their wartime experiences—polluted in a way that predisposed them to thoughtless violence. Ex-combatants were thought to have a blood lust and a propensity for erratic commission of violence. During my interview with

Esther, a psychosocial youth worker who was involved in rehabilitation with ex-combatants, she told me that she herself had fought in the war and related how she negotiated social stigma in the aftermath: "If you ex-combatant, you live in any community, for me—I will always give an example of myself. Where I live, people don't know that I fought war. Nobody know . . . because if they know I will feel embarrassed. People won't want to come around me. People won't want to feel free with me because they will feel that I ex-combatant. I killed. So anytime I can kill anybody. I can harm anybody. So you see?"

This was not an overblown assumption about how noncombatants perceived former fighters. While I was sitting with some of the young men in Red Light on a typically slow day, someone mentioned that a man in the community had recently beaten a child to death.

"A three years old child," Gibson kept repeating.

"The man was a former fighter," another piped up. "They get used to killing like that. They just like to see blood."

Popular conceptions of ex-combatants often feature assumptions about their having become "programmed killers" during the war, and remaining nothing more afterwards (see Denov 2010). The notion that ex-combatants had become programmed killing machines who liked to see blood was present on the local community level in Liberia as well. In the face of unexplainable behavior, speculations about how the war "spoiled" soldiers through drug addiction and bloodlust were tossed into social discourse like the example above.

Socialization into violence, which has been depicted as though it were outright "programming," is often assumed to be a cause for violence after war (see Achvarina and Reich 2006, 130). In her work in Uganda, Vermeij (2011) argues that socialization in the Lord's Resistance Army was a cause for ex-combatants' unconstrained commission of violence after leaving armed units. We should exercise caution in such an assessment. Though she defines "socialization" as a process by which naïve individuals are taught skills, values, and behaviors, and relates practices that the Lord's

Resistance Army used to train their recruits, she never actually provides a theorization of socialization as direct *cause* for behavior. Because she fails to situate her argument within a vast literature on the topic,[1] she problematically reifies notions of ex-combatants as "programmed killers."

Trauma is another, perhaps more prolific cause assumed to be behind aggressive and violent actions of former fighters after war—at the local level as well as in the literature. I heard this reasoning often and from the very first day of fieldwork. As we were driving from the airport the day I arrived I remember Daniel turning around in the car to talk about "our war-torn country." At one point he said, "The ex-combatants, some put their guns down with their hands, but not in their minds. They are traumatized." For him, and for so many others, this explained their criminal and violent behavior after the war.[2]

A vast literature tracks the psychological implications of exposure to, and participation in, violence (see Berman 2001; Gear 2002; Yule 2000). Quantities and qualities of exposure to violent acts, or commission of violence, have been associated with depression, anxiety, and post-traumatic stress disorder (PTSD), among other psychological disturbances (Bayer, Klansen and Adam 2007; Derluyn et al. 2004; Kanagaratnam, Raundalen, and Asbjørnsen 2005; Khort et al. 2010; Kuwert et al. 2008; Medeiros 2007). In particular, PTSD has been associated with increased instances of violent behavior (Norman 2014). In their comparative study of ex-combatants and noncombatants, Blattman and Annan (2010) find that ex-combatants have had higher rates of experience with and exposure to violence, and unsurprisingly this is associated with more numerous and difficult psychosocial implications after war.

Though experience with violence itself can hardly be contested as a cause of later difficulties, a number of scholars have challenged the "biomedical" approach of psychologists and psychiatrists who travel to postconflict countries and refugee camps to assess levels of disturbance. They cite limitations in reporting and a Western, "universalist" bias that informs the trauma paradigm as clear and problematic shortcomings of the biomedical paradigm (Bracken,

Giller, and Summerfield 1995; Eyber and Ager 2004; McKay and Wessells 2004; Summerfield 1999). Yet qualitative research with ex-combatants, conducted beyond the confines of diagnostic scales and indices, reveals instances of violent flashbacks—the sort that cause mental and emotional disturbance and have consequences for ex-combatants' ability to participate in relationships, or cause them to avoid certain areas associated with traumatic experience (Boothby 2006). I have not engaged the trauma discourse substantially, as I did not collect data regarding psychological history or experiences of disturbance. However, though the means and methods of assessing trauma may deserve intellectual scrutiny and some methodological improvement, the manifestation of trauma in ex-combatants' lives—as well as those of noncombatants—is not up for debate.

In terms of being "socialized" into violence a small pocket of research suggests that young people who are forced to perpetrate violence often come to enjoy it, to find it appealing and exciting (Elbert, Weierstall, and Schauer 2010). The research links "appetitive aggression" to early recruitment at young ages and to higher instances of perpetrated violence (Hecker et al. 2012; Weierstall et al. 2013). There is much to learn about this connection between early perpetration of violence and the enjoyment of violent aggression, and we should be extraordinarily careful not to overgeneralize assumptions about ex-combatants becoming killing machines who "like to see blood." Though their training and experience empowered and required them to perpetrate violence of various forms, there is no research that links participation in armed groups with prolific, ongoing postwar violence that is the result of some sort of cognitive reorganization. Once the militias were disbanded and the weapons, drugs, alcohol, and supplies were no longer organizing life and providing a purpose for violence, ex-combatants had much less incentive or opportunity to commit the kinds of violent acts they had perpetrated during the war.

While some ex-combatants like Esther negotiated ascribed identities as deviant and dangerous persons, other ex-combatants achieved the reputation that was applied more broadly to everyone. One night in the yard my friend Terry began to speak about his brother who had been recruited to fight with the NPFL as a small boy.

"My brother fought . . . my brother fought."

"He fought in the war?" I ventured carefully.

"Yes, he fought in the war. He is not encouraging us." He was referring to his family, particularly his siblings. He said his brother didn't want to do anything productive. He just wanted to take things. He did not care about anybody else. He said his brother drank a lot, and they were afraid of him. As he continued to speak I learned that the brother had stolen repeatedly from the family. He had taken his sister's laptop and held it for ransom. He returned it only after she agreed to pay him 100 U.S. dollars. He had been put in jail at one point, for allegedly beating a small child. I met the young man while visiting Terry's family. I slept with my own laptop in the bed with me that night, afraid that he would break in and attempt to steal my things.

Psychological work on trauma or aggression attends to changes in the individual's psyche. Theoretical work in this field would understand Terry's brother as having experienced psychological changes that resulted in his individual propensity to violate the trust and goodwill of his family. These are interpretations to which this research raises questions, but cannot rigorously address. What it can demonstrate is a social experience and adjustment that ex-combatants made in different ways as they negotiated changes in the postwar space.

Making Life through Violation

Ex-combatants are seen as a significant threat in the policy discourse. The breakup of factional networks is considered vital to postconflict security (see Spear 2002; UNDP 2011). If left together, armed groups are considered potential "spoilers" of postconflict peace. Frustrated ex-combatants who remain armed and organized might upset a fragile peace agreement. In his critical discourse analysis of the DDR process undertaken in Liberia, McMullin (2012, 390) argues that "the ex-combatant is constructed as a 'permanent outlaw' who represents a 'bundle of threats' unless he can be tempered by the post-conflict state under international tutelage." The aim of the demobilization, disarmament, and reintegration framework is to minimize security threats by occupying ex-combatants with education and job training, and removing as many weapons as possible. It is important that they have something "positive and constructive" to do, the UN (2010) asserts. As one aid worker commented in McMullin's (2013) work, vocational training is seen as something of a parking lot, a "holding position." It buys time for the consolidation of peace, regardless of whether it is actually effective in the lives of ex-combatants.

There is unquestionable evidence that ex-combatants can pose challenges to consolidation of postwar governance. In Liberia there is a well-documented instance in which several hundred ex-combatants took over the Guthrie Rubber Plantation, generating significant resources for their own purposes and posing a challenge to the state (see Cheng forthcoming; Persson 2012). By the time of my fieldwork, such "hot spots," as they are called, had diminished over time, in part due to the continued efforts made by the state and the international community to intervene and disrupt the power bases of these groups. Similarly, Lemasle (2010) observes that on a macro-level, patronage networks established in armed groups had significantly eroded by the time of her comparative study in Liberia and Sierra Leone.

Still, on a micro-level survival and respect could be managed among peers and patrons from the war. As I listened to ex-combatants talk about forming gangs after the war, it became apparent that these were not organizations of ideological opposition to the state. Gangs were social vehicles that preserved their recognition as big men and allowed them to make life through violation and violence, as they had done during the war. To go home to civilian families would require (most of) them to forfeit status they had earned during conflict. Sumo described this scenario quite well. After spending five days in the DDR cantonment camps, he was released, but he had no plans to return to his family.

"Well, when I was taken out of the [cantonment site], after five days I came out," he related. "I was given 150 USD. . . . If you come and take the gun from my hand, and just send me, to whom are you sending me to? . . . When we had the arm [gun] we feel we had power that we carry. So we felt that we was mature. So when the war subsided, and they took the arm from us, we felt shame. We felt too big to return to our parent' houses to be called 'baby.'"

Isaac explained this further. He was a local pastor who worked in rehabilitation with young ex-combatants. During his time working in an interim care center for former child soldiers he knew a young man who provides a stark contrast between the prestige of holding a gun during the war and the demotion that would occur if he were to reenter the household hierarchies in his parents' home.

"He told me, he said, 'I was a whole squad leader.' It meant he was a big man. 'I was a squad leader and if I go back to my parents they will ask me to go wash dishes, ask me to scrub the floor, ask me to wash their clothes.'" He was about fifteen years old when Isaac worked with him. At such an age these were tasks that a fifteen year old could reasonably expect to do.

"He said that he could not see himself going that road again. Out of the status that he had come from, out of the colonel rank, then seeing himself to go back to work to wash dishes, he said 'no.' He could not see himself to go back to it."

This is a well-established pattern among former fighters in postwar contexts. In Liberia, Utas (2005a) suggests that some former fighters choose not to go back to lives as civilians because this would "remarginalize" young men who had achieved status as big men, just as Isaac describes. In Mozambique, McMullin (2013, 8) relates a running joke among ex-combatants, as expressed by one man, "The government told us, 'Congratulations. Now you are all equally poor. You have been reintegrated back into basic poverty.'"

Ex-combatants like Sumo were uninterested in that sort of remarginalization. With factions disbanded in the months following the cease-fire, warlords like Taylor were no longer supplying their men. The ex-combatants were obliged to acquire drugs, alcohol, and food for themselves. From his "base," Sumo remembered running "operations" with his gang in Monrovia:

> I resulted to a high class criminal. . . . I was head of the armed robbery group here in Liberia. As a matter of fact, I controlled the entire Freeport at the time. . . . It was already known to me that police is nobody to me. Yeah, the police, other people, I consider them a subordinate. . . . My recruit, we move here and there. . . . I never remember [carrying out operations] in the night. All is broad day. I even remember some four years ago, I remember I arrived on Broad Street it was from in the morning to 12:00. Yes, and I wasn't arrested by any of the police. I always resisted. And under the Gyude Bryant government, two, three police were killed from me. . . . Ah, under this present government under which we are here, ah two got killed.

Years later, a former general came to him and encouraged him to stop. The teachings of Pentecostal Christianity were an integral part of his decision to put an end to the abuse and exploitation he had levied on the community with his gang. Sumo spoke at length about the spiritual teachings that gave new meaning to his life and his decision to desist from the violation of others and their property in Monrovia. At a social level, what is evident in his story is a renewed and redirected loyalty and allegiance to a big man from the war. This social attachment must not be missed. Everyone's ability to survive, belong, and be acknowledged with respect was bound up in their social networks. When young soldiers were incorporated into the ranks, their obligations to elders and to others were redirected to the ranks of their military organizations. After the war, they were told that their factions were no more, and to stop their way of life. Recall what David said about being a soldier man: "I violate at any time." Too "big" to go home, and unattached to the communities of noncombatants around them, many like Sumo continued to make life with their ex-combatant peers through the violent and violating means that were part of their everyday lives during the war. It took a relationship with someone that they respected to shift their orientation to the postwar space. In the following section, Randall's relationship with his family and then a former commander help to illustrate the importance that these relationships could have during difficult transitions.

Reorienting to Life without a Gun

Randall returned to a family who cared a great deal for his well-being. However, he struggled to negotiate social relations with noncombatants, and got into disagreements over money and interpersonal conduct on several occasions. He remembered that family imploring him to manage himself without causing trouble, and related some of the trouble that he caused. For example, at some point after the war he had been loaned a motorbike.

"Sometimes I would carry the bike two days, three days, myself I can be using it for my private use. I gave it to my friend and my friend went and sold it. He escaped. The [owner] said, 'I don't know the man you gave the bike to, but I know you. How you say you gave the bike to someone?'"

Randall's mother came to the owner and paid the value of the motorbike on Randall's behalf. "My mother came to pay 400 dollars U.S. to the man. The woman say, 'I must pay my money because my heart hurting me. So I can advise you. The thing you are doing, it bad on me, and you getting me? We gotta sit down and think. No more Charles Taylor business. Charles Taylor is not the one that born you—are you getting me? It only war came into this country and some of y'all took part inside. So long war, every day, but the war finish. Gotta sit down to think, gotta go back to school.'"

Randall never related exactly what he was using the motorbike for, but his mother's admonishment suggests that he was doing something of which she disapproved. At a more basic level, he had failed to be responsible for a costly vehicle that resulted in a great deal of expense for her.

"My mother called family meeting. Yeah, and she told me, 'don't go in jail. Don't look for problems. Because when you go in jail, myself I'm looking for it, eh? I beg you, don't get in problem. Take time with yourself in life."

She encouraged Randall to go back to school, to pick up where he had left off when he joined the NPFL in 1989. He had no patience for school, however, and left. His family communicated how much they wanted him to be all right, but eventually told him that they were at the end of their tether to know how to help him live and get along outside of "the Charles Taylor business" that had subsumed his life for so long. Eventually, he returned to the man he spoke about in chapter 5, the one who was like a godfather to him and his comrades.

"I came back to the man [commanding officer] I was with in the wartime," he related. "Because I don't have anybody, so he was assisting me. I used to drive for him also. During the wartime I used to drive for him. So he called me, and I was doing it—he do everything for me. He feed me, giving [to] me. . . . [It was] the same man that been with every one of us. . . . He brought us up during the crisis [the war]. We work for him, he like a godfather for us. That the man that take care of us, do everything for us. . . . I was not his son, nothing. But we had been together, serving one another life, and up to now we were able to live, to see the end. . . . I fall into trouble, he advise me. He said, 'You are not my son, but we fought war together. You must take time with yourself. Don't get into problem.'"

Serving one another's lives is an apt description of reciprocity. In a circumstance in which his family was unable to sustainably graft him into their lives, a former authority figure from the war *was* able to do so. He did it by offering Randall a socially acceptable livelihood and encouraging him not to make trouble for other people. They maintained their relationship as benefactor and dependent, and the respect that came with it. Similar circumstances emerged in numerous interviews with former commanding officers and soldiers. Instances like this one demonstrate that ex-combatants are not always or only "bundles" of threats. They are capable of wielding their influence and authority among their networks in ways that foster nonviolent social practices that are necessary for sustainable peace.

Separation and Intersection

Thus far, the life stories of Sumo and Randall may give the impression of rather fixed postwar trajectories, in which they continued to make life through violation until a turning point or conversion of some kind. When retold in this way, these turning points appear to alter completely the course of their lives, bringing them into socially acceptable modes of action within the postwar landscape. In the final section, Boima recounts a similar turning point. Part of this may be a result of memory, a product of hindsight, in which certain events signal changes that profoundly redirected their life courses. Some may have experienced very stark shifts as the result of relationships like the ones Sumo and Randall described. My time in Slipway, and among other ex-combatants in the city, suggests that major transitions were not so linear or so sudden for many ex-combatants. Rather, their willingness and ability to accommodate acceptable social norms and conduct among other Liberians could be disjointed and uncomfortable, a patchwork of their desire to assert themselves on their own terms blended together with attempts to do life as others would have them live. They did all this in an effort to maintain honor and prestige among one another as well as with noncombatants, most of whom regarded them with fear, skepticism, and at times deep contempt.

"The issue of stigma always making them to come together, to live together," Mary noted. A trained rehabilitation specialist, Mary had worked with a lot of ex-combatants in programs designed to help them reintegrate. "If you feel stigmatized, you always look for wherever you can find ex-combatants who will be somebody like you. I will tell you, 'at least I am safe to where I am.' You will want to join me. And I will start to call others from out there who will come and join."

Stigma was not only an issue because of acts of violence committed by ex-combatants in the aftermath of the ceasefire. Negative impressions of ex-combatants were also coupled with experiences that occurred *during* the war. Many Liberians could remember the soldiers who hurt them or their loved ones. On occasion, perpetrators and victims ran into each other. Memories of the past were carried into present exchanges that resulted in immense discomfort for both parties. Violent and abusive experiences that induced fear and harm for victims during the war could turn to resentment in the aftermath.

One of my neighbors recalled a vivid example of this kind of encounter. During the early years of the crisis soldiers were going house to house, killing anyone they suspected of being Americo. Suspicion was enough reason for the soldiers to fire on the spot. My neighbor Josephine and her aunty fled the house, her small son strapped to her back. On their way up the street a young soldier stopped them and threatened them at gunpoint. Her aunty dropped the things she was carrying. Feeling faint, Josephine nearly fell backwards, and her son began to slide from her back. She caught him by his leg. Seeing her struggle, a man rushed from behind to help her with her son. The soldier boy shot him in cold blood.

Years later, after the war, the very same young man occasionally passed through Josephine's yard to go to a shop on the other side of her property. One day she stopped him as he and some friends were passing through. "Do you know me?" The young man said "No." She asked him again, "Do you know me?" He replied "No," again, adding that he met lots of people. She recalled to him the day he threatened her, the woman with the baby on her back, and the man that he shot. He asked her to please put it in the past. Things had changed. His friends encouraged him to be nice to her, telling him that if she were a wicked woman she would find him and poison him in revenge. He never passed through her yard again.

Most ex-combatants chose to live with one another. Pockets of ex-combatant communities were peppered all throughout the greater Monrovia area, and people knew where they were. Faction affiliations were common and groups often clustered around a big man from the war. Interestingly, having been a fighter in the civil war was enough to draw ex-combatants together. Young men from different, opposing factions became members of the same ex-combatant communities. Shared social identities as ex-combatants—even from opposing sides—became the tie that bound them together. Clumped in ghettos and residential areas and living separately from others reaffirmed the distinction between themselves as men and women from war and others who were not a part of their wartime lives or experience.

Slipway was such a community. It was notorious in a way that raised eyebrows when I mentioned to my neighbors that I was spending time there. "You're a real tough guy!" Tee exclaimed when she heard where I had been going during the day. "Even I wouldn't go there," she continued. "I know where to look over from the car. But I wouldn't go in."

Liberians expected ex-combatants to be loud, rowdy, sometimes rude and aggressive. They were known for drinking and smoking and careless if not reckless behavior. Drug use and violence were expected in their enclaves, and people like my neighbors preferred not to enter ex-combatant spaces.

Though ex-combatants found support among one another in these communities, most places like Slipway were not self-sustaining enough to exist without interaction with the wider urban community. Ex-combatants needed jobs. Slipway was in desperate need of water and road repair. A former general named Brutus was a leader in Slipway and one of my first contacts. His attempt to leverage resources, assert his prestige as a big man, and protect his honor as a husband demonstrate the disjointed patchwork of social practice that converged in social interactions and across social spaces.

Our relationship developed over the months that I visited the community, and eventually there was a community celebration that he invited me to. All of the women were wearing the same print, which I obtained and had a dress made from. The president's son Robert Sirleaf was supposed to be there to see the community, a point that Brutus was immensely proud of. That day he wore a three-piece suit and spoke to the crowd with the demeanor of a statesman. He was a big man. The president's son had arranged to have some public works done in Slipway, and he was the social link in the chain of resources from the government. We took pictures in our fine outfits, and celebrated the new developments that would help the community. In all of this, Brutus was asserting his prestige in Slipway. He had obtained a position of leadership and authority over others, one in which he was working with the government that had overthrown Charles Taylor—his former warlord and leader. He had adapted to the new conditions in the country, and been willing to accommodate a new regime. All of this suggested significant shifts in his allegiance to a new system of authority and a different way of doing life after guns.

Though this kind of social practice illustrates adjustment to "acceptable" postwar life, he could also exemplify the deeply ingrained stereotypes that fueled the stigma associated with ex-combatants. One morning not long after the community celebration I rode over to Slipway. I bought Brutus a big beer, and we shared it with several other men in a little hutch that was made for shelter from the sun. It was not yet noon, but Brutus was already feeling the affects of previously consumed alcohol, if not also marijuana. I wondered if his intoxication would prove a barrier to other conversations I had looked forward to having. I had just settled into a glass of beer, and Brutus's slurred, unrelenting monologue about something in the community, when a young police officer came by and sat down to speak with him. The day before there was "confusion" (conflict) between Brutus and an elderly gentleman.

"Abby, this man . . . ," Brutus began to relate. "This man . . ." He explained that the older man had gotten on a megaphone the day before, and said all kinds of things about Brutus in the community, especially how he had been loving to another woman that was not his wife. In outrage, Brutus called the police and had the older man thrown in jail. In the midst of his inebriated recounting of the story, Brutus rattled off his wedding date to all of us who were sitting in the little hutch. "Legally married!," he kept exclaiming in defense of his honor as a husband. "Legally married!," he continued, noting the cost of his wife's wedding dress, and how he had ordered it and had it brought over from the United States. Meanwhile, since the older man's accusations over the megaphone the day before, Brutus's wife had been unhappy with him, which was a problem. He insisted that his honor had been impugned and that they settle the matter formally, in court.

What happened next was a paradox, in which Brutus insisted on clearing his honor through increasingly dishonorable forms of conduct. The conversation in the little hutch escalated quickly. Suddenly the group of us was walking across the street to the police depot, where Brutus demanded that they bring the old man out. He was brought out, quiet and handcuffed, gray stubble poking through his leathery chin. Brutus made a scene. There was a lot of shouting and shoving, and Brutus was in the middle of it until finally he got his way. They put the old man, still handcuffed, onto a motorbike and we all rode over to the court in West Point, a neighboring community where there was a small court in which Brutus insisted that his honor as a husband be vindicated.

At the courthouse Brutus continued to be loud and ornery while he was waiting to be seen by the judge. At some point he had an exchange with an elderly lawyer who was in the waiting area. He insulted the man, who had somehow offended him, and proclaimed, "I am a friend of the president's son!"

"Then why do you disgrace the name of the president by behaving in this way?," the lawyer queried him.

"Shut up!," Brutus spat back. "Shut up!"

The scandalous rebuke of an elder in that way had everyone imploring Brutus to desist. Brutus tried to pick a verbal argument with the older lawyer, demanding that he come outside for palaver. The older man ignored him, calmly pulling his coat on, "behaving like that . . . ," he muttered softly as he left the building.

The ruckus subdued when the judge brought Brutus in. He was calm, and looked at Brutus squarely. "I don't like to be disrespected in this chair," he said. "You have liquor on your breath. I drink liquor, but not when I'm here. And I don't hear people who are under the influence. You're under the influence." He continued along that vein for a little while, telling Brutus that he couldn't reason well, and that he was being loud and emotional because of the liquor. "I can smell it on you. I can smell it on you." The second point, he said, is that "you have brought an old man. If it was a younger man, I might have heard the case. But you have brought an older man. What could this man have done so bad to you? You are the leader of that organization in the community. The leader," he kept reiterating. "What could this man have done so bad to you? Is your skin that thin?"

Somewhat contrite at this stage, Brutus tried to interject, starting with how the man impugned his honor by saying he had been loving to another woman. The judge stopped him: "I'm not here to hear that today. You got liquor on your breath. Go back, try to resolve it in the community. You couldn't resolve this thing in the community?"

With that, the judge threw the case out. Exhausted from the amount of relational conflict I was not accustomed to, I flagged down a motorbike and rode home.

When I retold the story over beers in the yard that evening, it rang true for my friends as the rowdy stereotype of ex-combatants misbehaving in their own community, and elsewhere. Brutus had been rude, and verbally and physically aggressive. Worst of all, he had dragged an older man to jail and then to court, and while there he had maligned another man who had not offended him at all. It was a severe offense to disrespect one's elders in such a way.

This evocative account of respect and disrespect is multilayered and rich with contradictions that reflect the complexity of postwar social relations. There are a couple of themes that are especially important for this work. First, this episode demonstrates how blended ex-combatants' social conduct could be. Brutus's early morning boozing and bullheaded actions were indicative of the pollutant Flomo talked about. His alcohol-infused behavior was a testament of the remnant of the child soldier, amoral and disregarding of the norms and values on which the society was built. He had acted out the stereotype that most ex-combatants were saddled with after the war.

Knowing him as I did, the whole fiasco was more complicated. It demonstrated a disjointed attempt to preserve his honor by adhering to competing codes of respect. On the one hand, he asserted himself over the elderly gentleman—and insulted another—with no regard for the gerontocratic position they held in society. This harks back to the kinds of conduct armed soldiers displayed with noncombatant elders during the war. Their value to society was not recognized by many armed groups, leading to the kinds of memories that the older gentleman related in the previous chapter. Brutus's behavior resembles the same kind of disregard for social values regarding the elderly. It demonstrates that he has not fully realigned himself to the accepted codes of conduct—as Randall and Sumo appear to do in the earlier sections. At the same time, however, he was very fixated on nonviolent, formal means of vindication. He chose to have the police and the court system involved, rather than choose violent or violating means of asserting power over his elderly accuser. All of this was in an attempt to clear his name as a husband to a wife who had been with him during the war and who had remained with him afterward. He introduced me to her proudly on one of my earliest visits. "She been with me since the war," he smiled. She had smiled too at that statement, and they pulled out pictures of their son, boasted of his school achievements, and showed me photos of their wedding. The whole event of jailing his elderly accuser and taking him to court appeared to me as a disjointed attempt to preserve his honor through formal postwar institutions, while failing to comply with one of the most significant social values—respecting the position of one's elders.

Some might see his disrespect for both elders in this story as evidence that armed groups inverted gerontocratic norms during the war, and continued to act that way afterwards. I would contend that neither of these gentlemen was in his network of hierarchical reciprocity. His behavior with them demonstrated an ongoing relational break with the larger society—one that he is seeking to bridge in part by using formal court systems set up by the postwar state.

Second, this instance demonstrates a far more contentious and complicated adjustment to life after guns, a kind of uneven and patchy transition, where movement in and out of ex-combatant enclaves is not so fluid or seamless as the account of Sumo and Randall might lead us to believe. While they describe very linear trajectories out of the "Charles Taylor business" and ways of life, Brutus acts in contradictory ways in an effort to assert his prestige over the older man and preserve his honor. It is messy and difficult, and not clear cut.

Some weeks later I invited Brutus and Sekou, who featured in the previous chapter, to my neighborhood where my friends were throwing a going-away party for me. My own neighbors would not have dared to venture into their community in Slipway, but they were tenuously welcomed to ours. Brutus brought his wife and another friend, and they came and celebrated with us. They were smiling and friendly. They chatted with other people. No one was too loud, too drunk, or "inappropriate" in any way.

Reciprocity and Respect in Families

In this final section I draw from Boima's postwar story. His postwar transition represents some of the primary trends among young men who "put the gun down in their minds," and were able to do so in no small part through the relationships they reestablished with families, kin, and within communities. Initially, when the war ended, Boima continued to perpetrate violence and crime, much like Sumo described.

He remembered, "During those years [before the war ended in 2003] my life was all right, because I was depending on the arm [gun]. And after then, we had properties that we looted, and we were sustaining ourselves with it. So I was living good life. But for now we know that the life we were living was not a good life. Because we forcibly take things from people, we did things to people, and, you know, to make people feel bad. And we discouraged people. And we ourselves, we were discouraged in life too."

Importantly, and not to be minimized, despite notable and prolific critiques of the UN DDR process, Boima responded favorably to the programs implemented with ex-combatants. He, like many other former fighters, spoke well of the counseling he received.

"We came for disarmament. That how the UN came into the country. When the UN came, that how they disarm us. So some of us decided to go for disarmament. I was disarmed in Buchanan. I was disarmed and they compensated me $150 U.S. People came. People came to counsel us. We had a counselor who came to us from the UN. Some people who hold gun [ex-combatants], they came to talk to us, to convince us that what we were doing was not good. And we ourselves began to realize, our own knowledge began to open, we began to realize that what we were doing was not nice. So we decided to desist from it."

For Boima, at least in his remembrance of that period in his life, there was an "ah-hah" moment during the DDR counseling. For Sumo, a similar turning point came through accepting the teaching of a Pentecostal preacher. In other instances, ex-combatants did not express such responses to teaching or rehabilitation of one kind or another. Randall's transition to socially acceptable relationships and modes of action in the postconflict period occurred over time, as he bumped into trouble over money, caused strife in his family, and eventually reattached himself to someone he respected. Also important for Randall, his former commander was able to supply him with an acceptable livelihood as a driver. In Boima's case, the livelihood training he received through the DDR process was effective.

"After three months, when they call, we get another 150 U.S.," he explained. "That three hundred dollars. They asked everybody if they wanted to go to school, if you want to learn trade. Anything you decide to do, you can do it. I decide to do trade. So now I do general construction. Yeah, that what I decide to do. Yeah, so I can build house [that can repel or keep out water], I can bring it up to level. Roofing, plastering, I can do it, and you can pay me what I ask you. That what I learn after the war. That how I living now."

Boima's response, both to the counseling and the vocational training provided through the DDR process, is a best case scenario, and one that was not experienced by many of his peers. They took the money given to them for the purpose of investing in their newly acquired livelihood skills, and spent it on other things. Sumo recalled going straight to the ghetto. "We brought the money, and—for me, I didn't even reach my own, my house . . . I was in the ghetto. I already finish all." Ex-combatants were also known for selling tools provided in vocational school, rendering their training rather ineffective without the instruments to build houses, run pipelines, or grow crops.

In her extensive work with former child and youth soldiers in Sierra Leone, Shepler (2014) argues that skills training was rarely if ever enough to provide young people with sustainable livelihoods. She suggests that apprenticeships in intergenerational hierarchies were more socially acceptable, and grafted young people into relationships that society could understand and approve of. Some of the ex-combatants in Liberia were apprenticed, with rehabilitation workers recalling varying levels of success. Regardless of being formally apprenticed, what seems most important is that ex-combatants have personal networks that trust them and will patronize their business. As long as stigma inhibits the trust of the wider community, ex-combatants are likely to struggle for their daily bread, regardless of how appropriate their skills training is to the demands of the market. They will have only their networks from war, which are unlikely to provide enough for subsistence, especially if so many of them earned the same skills and vie for opportunities where demand is already low.

What made the difference in Boima's case was his integration with his family, relationships in which he could earn social honor in their eyes and in the eyes of his community. Boima was the head of his house, the breadwinner, and the responsible son who took care of an elderly father.

"I got four children. I even got my woman living with me," he told me proudly. "My father, everyone . . . For now, everything I'm doing for now, it's for my children. I'm not doing it for myself. For me now, I got my own place. I'm not depending on anybody now. I'm only depending on myself. I lose my mother three years ago. I only got my father now, living. I supporting him now. Now, I have learned something to sustain my family. . . . The life we are living today is a good life, because now we sweat for what we get at the end of the day."

The ex-combatants who were involved in their family systems were proud of their relationships, roles, and responsibilities. I was introduced to parents and children. They proudly emphasized their accomplishments within their families, be it supporting elderly parents or paying for children's school fees. As Boima pointed out, he was responsible to care for and support not only his wife and his children but also his father. He was fully embedded within the accepted intergenerational hierarchies that organized Liberian family life. He spoke repeatedly of being called for construction jobs in his community, of how others recommended him for work.

"We decide for no war to be in our country again," Boima said. "Yeah, for now, we just relax, we don't have no problem with nobody. Because of what we have achieved, and what we living for now."

Conclusion

Reintegration is social more than vocational. In a context organized by hierarchical networks of patrons and clients, and in which there were not nearly enough jobs—formal or informal—one's networks of support were far more important than vocational skills. Boima's ability to capitalize on his training had everything to do with his social networks in the community. Without them, he would have been in a similar position to Ben or David, struggling to find shelter, out of work, and frustrated by their inability to make a life. Horizontal transitions out of armed groups were not as direct or clear-cut coming out of the war as going in. Ex-combatants negotiated, and sometimes played into, varying degrees of stigma from families and communities that strongly influenced their transitions within the postwar terrain, much of which revolved around making life and maintaining respect within social relations, be they with former fighters, families, or some combination.

Utas (2008) suggests that vertical transitions downward to lower socioeconomic status made for an experience of abjection, of being "thrown down." I would add that the abjection felt related not only to losing social status in the vertical sense but also to their horizontal transitions out of armed groups and into an ambiguous postwar terrain, where to whom and to what they were supposed to transition was not straightforward. The armed groups that had organized and sustained their lives disbanded, their communities and families regarded them with varying levels of acceptance and rejection, and subsistence was a struggle. Many like Ben expressed feelings of abjection that resonate with Jackson's (2006) articulation of being ground down in an environment where their agency appeared to be largely in the hands of others. Those who did not express abjection in this way had been able, like Randall and Boima, to maintain respect as social honor—if not also prestige—through interdependent networks of support.

7
Conclusion
On Dominance and Discourse

I set out to provide an ethnographic sketch of actors in context, one that would render a fuller appreciation of the social contours in which these young men make life in the aftermath of war. My aim was to challenge and inform a limited and pejorative binary about youth as damaged or damaging. One of the principal errors of such dichotomies is that they fixate on violence as it is received or dealt at the site of the individual person, or in this case a gender and generation, ignoring and obscuring broader systems of violence at work across groups and built up over time. This book speaks most directly to the notion that young people pose particular risks to fragile environments. If I have been successful, the reader will leave with a more nuanced sense of context and structure in postwar Monrovia, and with questions and observations about how young men fit into local, national, and international configurations of power and possibility.

This research contributes to scholarship in youth studies in a couple of important ways. It situates youth as far more nestled within intergenerational relations than they often appear in the literature. It gives us a fuller grasp of their social positions among family and kin and how those relationships affect their life chances and transitions. This is particularly relevant among ex-combatants. DDR policy and programs stress skills training and education as vital components of sustainable transitions to life outside of armed groups. While vocational training can be useful, as in Boima's case, the young men in the study make it clear that networks of reciprocity and indebtedness are precursors to jobs and livelihoods.

I want to conclude this book with several reflections about dominance and dignity and structural reproduction. I argued that the war was not caused by a demographic overabundance of violent young men, greed, or grievance, but rather by a legacy of dominance that denied dignity within the country, and that can be traced all the way back to the slave trade in the United States. The dominant white landowners and slave owners in the United States set the terms by which some people could be valued as civilized. They decided who could be *human* enough to be worthy of an equal place in American society. People of color were deemed unworthy. When free black men, women and children journeyed across the Atlantic to West Africa, ideas about who was civilized and what was civilized were not reconfigured or challenged, but instead transplanted, resown like seeds in the new nation of Liberia, fortifying the dominance of the Americo elite and the structural subjection of the indigenous majority. Chapter 3 illustrates how the structural dominance of the Americo elite resurfaced in the social norms and values espoused by postwar young men. The only way to get ahead was to assimilate into Americo criteria for sociocultural life, and to achieve the U.S.-based credentials that were at their disposal, and completely unattainable to the vast majority. The historical continuity of the class divide is particularly visible in the national coat of arms, an emblem attached to nearly all official government business. It still reads at the time of this writing "The love of liberty brought *us* here" (emphasis added). The perpetuation of structural inequality throughout their history as a nation suggests that as long as the Americo minority set the agenda, the majority of Liberians will likely struggle to feel ownership of a country where "love of liberty" brought *others* to their shores, or to feel worthy of a place in their country.

Similarly, the structural dominance of former slave-owning and colonial powers in the West has been reproduced, as evidenced by the "loose molecules paradigm"—which is really just an extension of the New Barbarism applied specifically to young men. Unable (perhaps unwilling?) to comprehend wars like those waged across the continent, proponents of the New Barbarism concept ascribe armed conflict to the primal nature of black Africans. In postconflict settings, the viability of a sustainable peace is dependent upon the successful management of young people and ex-combatants, who are presumably—by nature—predisposed to instigating and perpetuating violence. In so doing, this underlying paradigm reinforces the distinction between the kinds of people who need to be managed and the kinds of people who should manage them.

McMullin (2012, 2013) effectively identifies this discourse in the threat narrative that pervades DDR policy and practice within the United Nations and their institutional partners. The research in this book demonstrates that similar appropriations of young men are reproduced within the country itself, and among young men's own communities. The weight of stigma was a significant burden both to ex-combatant and noncombatant youth. This is where a theoretical interpretation of structure, agency, and structural reproduction becomes so critical. If we assert that underlying values and norms form the basis for social relations and the distribution of power within them, and that it is through enactment of those core assumptions and evaluations, through agency, that the structure of society, local and global, is reproduced over time, then all actors are co-contributors to the remaking or reformulating of structure. Agents at local and global levels have reasserted a discourse of youth as troublesome and violent, perpetuating not just the stigma around youth but the occlusion of structural violence at all levels.

One of the primary critiques of this theoretical approach is in its duality. Structure informs agency, agency bolsters structure, and the two perpetually reinforce one another in a rather deterministic cycle. My argument over the course of this book emphasizes that duality, as I have mainly highlighted the reproduction of dominance versus any sort of substantial change in the Liberian case. That is why Joshua's assessment of his livelihood as a drug dealer is so intriguing and illuminating. As long as the dominant cultural fraction sets the terms by which dignity could be achieved, young men like Timothy and his friends in Red Light will struggle for worthiness. Joshua presented a more liberated assessment of himself, far less burdened by the stigma Timothy expressed. Recall Timothy's words about smoking marijuana: "A real mother will not accept her child doing drugs. So you won't be with your parents and doing it." Yet Joshua's mother did accept her child, and affirmed his effort to support himself. She reformulated the terms by which Joshua could be valued, and her assessment was the one that really mattered to him. I raise this circumstance not to advocate for parental promotion of drug dealing but as an observation of discourse at work in a young person's life. It is an example of how discourse can imbue or inhibit dignity. It is an insight about in whose eyes one is considered worthy or found wanting. As long as the dominant view was the most important, young men like Timothy and Joshua would not measure up. The criteria for worthiness were largely out of their reach. Dignity is ultimately claimed by achieving worth in the eyes of those considered the most worthy—whether that is one's mother, one's self, or one's community. And if it is over dignity that wars such as this one are fought, then the ultimate battleground is one of discourse, in which dominant views regarding social worth are challenged in everyday life, in the law, in the media, in research, and in theory.

At a large scale I have argued that the underlying cause for the Liberian civil war shows strong signs of remaking itself in the years since the cease-fire. Are Liberia and other lower income countries submerged in a perpetual, and deterministic, cycle of oppression and inequality? Regarding structural duality Sewell (1992) suggests that structural change can happen for a number of reasons. Among them, he observes that when resources become scarcer or more abundant, the balance of power in society is likely to shift. If structural contexts overlap or converge they are prone to inform and question one another and the practice of everyday life. With these and other instances, Sewell is getting at the significance of experience—experience of something new, of something different, of some kind of change. With that experience comes the opportunity to reassess, to alter, or to reconfigure the values and norms that form the foundation for agency—for the reproduction or alteration of the world in which we live. Lubkemann (2008) asserts that wars are an opportunity to do just that. Joshua and his mother appear to have taken that opportunity in their own lives and in their relationship with each other. That opportunity to reassess the terms by which we value one another exists at national and international levels, too, where the underlying prejudices held by our collectives shape the economic and political decisions taken between and across continents, and with sweeping affects for the everyday lives of our fellow human beings.

I argue that the war in Liberia was caused by dominance exercised not just by the Americo elite, but that it had roots in the United States, where the "civilizing" project to remove freed slaves was ultimately an attempt to manage the problem of slavery. Getting rid of free men and women of color was easier than taking responsibility for their degradation and integrating them as equals. Strains of that prejudice so evident in the eighteenth and nineteenth centuries persist in the New Barbarism, the loose molecules paradigm, and the threat narrative that scapegoats young men as causes of violence and upheaval. As long as young men and the countries where they live are viewed in this way, they will always need help and management, and the dominant global fraction in the West can be reasserted through pejorative discourses about "the other." Dominance bestows and denies dignity within national borders and on a global scale. The history of this small West African nation demonstrates that ideas about the other fuel structural violence and lay the foundation for deadly conflict. As long as these destructive, essentializing stereotypes persist, so too will inequality, the denial of dignity, and the opportunity for armed conflict.

Acknowledgments

I am humbled by the community of people acknowledged below and by countless others who went out of their way to lend a helping hand from the beginning of this project to its end. I feel I must also acknowledge that whatever contributions this work makes to theory, practice, or personal reflection, no one has benefited from this opportunity more than I. Living and learning in Liberia and in Oxford has transformed the way that I understand the world and my place in it. I am so grateful.

In Liberia, I must express my deepest gratitude to my hosts and my family in Matadi. Kona, Korpo, Tenne, TJ, and Jessica, your helping hand has made a lasting impact on this book and on my life. Thank you. A big shout out to mini Abby! Very special thanks are due to Chara Itoka and to Morlee Zawoo, your thoughts and guidance were anchors for me. Sam Clawson, thanks for being my friend. I would also like to thank Jerry Kandea, Chris Lang, John Moniba, Pastor Success, Michael "I Mean It", and Pastor Johnson.

In the United Kingdom, I cannot imagine doing this research outside of the Loft at the Department of International Development at the University of Oxford. I am deeply grateful to a community of minds and hearts who challenged and supported my work and my person on a daily basis. To a clump of you, I am especially thankful for anchoring me. To Asha Amirali, Narae Choi, Nadiya Figueroa, Neil Howard, Elise Klein, Alex Lowe, James Morrissey, Taylor St. John, and Cameron Thibos, you have lit my life with such joy, tenderness, and love, each in your own way, and as a collective. Thank you. Zoe Marks, you can understand from a special vantage point, and I have taken such comfort in that.

Thanks also to Liz Cooper, Marco DiNunzio, Gina Crivello, and Ginny Morrow: your input on earlier drafts of this work was so constructive and formative.

In the United States, to my community at Thinking Beyond Borders, fellow sojourners and askers of difficult questions, your enthusiasm for and encouragement of this book have meant a great deal to me. Special thanks to Elena Rae for nudging me to stay present with myself in the final stages of writing. To Tessa, Helen, Vern, and Janita, I could not have asked for a sweeter community in which to complete the final book draft. To my mom, who was my first writing coach, and who generously proofread every draft chapter of this book, thank you for investing. To my dad, brother, and sister, your interest and encouragement mean so much. On James Hill, Laura, James, and Mary, thank you for keeping me grounded!

Finally, I am grateful to the anonymous reviewers for their attention to this manuscript. I would like to thank especially Joss Alexander and Mats Utas for treating the earlier version of this book with the constructive care that has encouraged its development to publication. I would not have written a book at all had it not been for the visionary support of Lynda Walters, who encouraged my transition to Development Studies at Oxford. The catalyst for all of this was a copy of *Reader's Digest*, picked up at the eye doctor so long ago. I am grateful to Angelina Jolie for that—who would've thought? In all of this, I owe an immense debt of gratitude to Jo Boyden. Your unwavering support of my growth and my work has been a firm foundation for so many years. Thank you for pushing me to own it and do it with the best of my abilities. I have grown immeasurably under your guidance.

Notes

Chapter 1. Introduction

1. I use the term "Global South" sparingly, and with some reservation, to refer to smaller countries outside of the West. I use it in lieu of reference to their state of "development," or their position in a first, second, or third place lineup—both of which assume a hierarchy that requires a great deal of unpacking.
2. The ex-combatant occupation of the Guthrie Plantation is a prime example; see Cheng forthcoming and Persson 2012.
3. An example can be seen on page 14 of the UNDP 2003–2004 Activity Report.

Chapter 2. A History of Violence

1. See Bourgois's (2009) working definition for structural violence, accompanied by definitions of symbolic and normalized violence.
2. There were 697,624 at the first census taken in 1790, see U.S. census report "Statistics of Slaves" at http://www2.census.gov/prod2/decennial/documents/00165897ch14.pdf.
3. See Levitt (2005) for a thorough and analytical review of the conflicts between various tribes and the American settlers in Liberia.
4. "The Planting Agreement of 1926" can be found in its entirety in Buell's (1947) appendix 5.
5. Taken from a census quoted in Reno 1998.

6. For example, see Boley's (1983) long list of Tolbert's appointments of family members to public office. See Liebenow's (1962) chart for an earlier example of the kinship ties that crossed extensively through local and national level political positions.

Chapter 4. Street Youth

1. This was less than four and a half U.S. dollars at the time Washington related the story.
2. This is a conflation similarly observed in Abramowitz's (2014) work in Liberia.
3. Fieldnote, February 14, 2010.
4. Fieldnote, March 7, 2011.

Chapter 5. Life in Armed Groups

1. I am borrowing Stewart's (2008) use of horizontal to think across groups, and vertical to indicate differences in status between people.
2. One use for the word "embarrass" in Liberia—the use being applied here—is to hurt or cause great discomfort. It is a stronger meaning than to make someone shy.
3. See the 1997 issue of *Africa Development* 22 (3–4).
4. For more thorough and detailed accounts of the Poro and of bush school, see Bellman (1984), Fulton (1972), Little (1965, 1966), and Welmers (1949).
5. From his work with the Kpelle, Welmers (1949) relates a wide range of meanings for "medicine" (*sále*) that could include substances, utterances, actions, and even organizations that were believed to possess unusual powers. Medicines could be curative or contaminating—so poisons were also called medicine.
6. Marks (2013) relates that looting was implemented by the Revolutionary United Front as a regular strategy for feeding the troops.

Chapter 6. Life after Guns

1. To name only a few, see work on social learning theory (Bandura 1977; Bandura, Ross, and Ross 1961; Sutherland 1956), social control (Hirschi 1969; Hirschi and Gottfredson 1995), violent and impoverished environments (Stewart, Simons, and Conger 2001), and socialization for aggression, war, and violence (Bandura 1980; Ember and Ember 2007).
2. See Abramowitz (2014) for an analysis of the trauma discourse in the postwar years.

References

Abdullah, I. 1997. "Bush Path to Destruction: The Origin and Character of the Revolutionary United Front (RUF/SL)." *Africa Development* 22 (3–4): 45–76.

Abramowitz, S. A. 2014. *Searching for Normal in the Wake of the Liberian War*. Philadelphia: University of Pennsylvania Press.

Achvarina, V., and S. F. Reich. 2006. "No Place to Hide: Refugees, Displaced Persons and the Recruitment of Child Soldiers." *International Security* 31 (1): 127–164.

Agamben, G. 1999. *Remnants of Auschwitz: The Witness and the Archive*. New York: Zone Books.

Bandura, A. 1977. *Social Learning Theory*. Englewood Cliffs, NJ: Prentice-Hall.

———. 1980. "The Social Learning Theory of Aggression." In *The War System: An Interdisciplinary Approach*, edited by R. A. Falk and S. S. Kim. Boulder: Westview Press.

Bandura, A., D. Ross, and S. A. Ross. 1961. "Transmission of Aggression through Imitation of Aggressive Models." *Journal of Abnormal and Social Psychology* 63 (3): 575–582.

Bayer, C. P., F. Klansen, and H. Adam. 2007. "Association of Trauma and PTSD Symptoms with Openness to Reconciliation and Feelings of Revenge among Former Ugandan and Congolese Child Soldiers." *Journal of American Medical Association* 298: 555–559.

Bellman, B. L. 1984. *The Language of Secrecy: Symbols and Metaphors in Poro Ritual*. New Brunswick: Rutgers University Press.

Berman, H. 2001. "Children and War: Current Understandings and Future Directions." *Public Health Nursing* 18 (4): 243–252.

Blattman, C. 2009. "From Violence to Voting: War and Political Participation in Uganda." *American Political Science Review* 103: 231–247.

Blattman, C., and J. Annan. 2010. "The Consequences of Child Soldiering." *Review of Economics and Statistics* 92: 882–898.

———. 2011. "Reintegrating and Employing High-Risk Youth in Liberia: Lessons from a Randomized Evaluation of a Landmine Action Agricultural Training Program for Ex-Combatants." New Haven, CT: Innovations for Poverty Action and Yale University.

———. "Can Employment Reduce Lawlessness and Rebellion? A Field Experiment with High-Risk Men in a Fragile State." *American Political Science Review* 110 (1): 1–17.

Bledsoe, C. 1980. *Women and Marriage in Kpelle Society*. Stanford: Stanford University Press.

———. 1990. "'No Success without Struggle': Social Mobility and Hardship for Foster Children in Sierra Leone." *Man*, n.s., 25 (1): 70–88.

———. 1993. "The Politics of Polygymy in Mende Education and Child Fosterage." In *Sex and Gender Hierarchies*, edited by B. D. Miller. New York: Cambridge University Press.

Bøås, M. 2001. "Liberia and Sierra Leone—Dead Ringers? The Logic of Neopatrimonial Rule." *Third World Quarterly* 22 (5): 697–723.

Bøås, M., and A. Hatløy. 2008. "'Getting In, Getting Out': Militia Membership and Prospects for Re-integration in Post-War Liberia." *Journal of Modern African Studies* 46: 33–55.

Boersch-Supan, J. 2009. *What the Communities Say: The Crossroads between Integration and Reconciliation: What Can Be Learned from the Sierra Leonean Experience?* CRISE Working Paper No. 63. Oxford: Centre for Research on Inequality, Human Security, and Ethnicity.

Boley, G. E. S. 1983. *Liberia: The Rise and Fall of the First Republic*. London: Macmillan.

Boothby, N. 2006. "What Happens When Child Soldiers Grow Up? The Mozambique Case Study." *Intervention* 4 (3): 244–259.

Boothby, N., J. Crawford, and J. Halperin. 2006. "Mozambique Child Soldier Life Outcome Study: Lessons Learned in Rehabilitation and Reintegration Efforts." *Global Public Health* 1: 87–107.

Bourdieu, P. 1977. *Outline of a Theory of Practice*. Cambridge: Cambridge University Press.

———. 1986. "The Forms of Capital." In *Handbook of Theory and Research for the Sociology of Education*, edited by J. E. Richardson. New York: Greenwood Press.

Bourgois, P. 2003. *In Search of Respect: Selling Crack in El Barrio.* 2nd ed. New York: Cambridge University Press.

———. 2009. "Recognizing Invisible Violence: A Thirty-Year Ethnographic Retrospective." In *Global Health in Times of Violence*, edited by Barbara Rylko-Bauer, Linda Whiteford, and Paul Farmer. Santa Fe: School of American Research Press.

Boyden, J. 2007. "Children, War and World Disorder in the 21st Century: A Review of the Theories and the Literature on Children's Contributions to Armed Violence." *Conflict, Security, and Development* 7: 255–279.

Bracken, P., J. E. Giller, and D. Summerfield. 1995. "Psychological Responses to War and Atrocity: The Limitations of Current Concepts." *Social Science & Medicine* 40: 1073–1082.

Bragg, C. 2006. *Challenges to Policy and Practice in the Disarmament, Demobilisation, Reintegratiuon and Rehabilitation of Youth Combatants in Liberia.* Sussex Migration Working Paper 29. Brighton: University of Sussex Centre for Migration Research.

Buell, R. L. 1947. *Liberia: A Century of Survival 1847–1947*. Philadelphia: University of Pennsylvania Press, the University Museum.

Chabal, P. 2009. *Africa: The Politics of Suffering and Smiling*. London: Zed Books.

Cheney, K. E. 2005. "'Our Children Have Only Known War': Children's Experiences and the Uses of Childhood in Northern Uganda." *Children's Geographies* 3: 23–45.

Cheng, C. Forthcoming. *Post-Conflict Transitions and Extralegal Groups.* Oxford: Oxford University Press.

Christoffersen, K. 2010. "Disarming and Reintegrating Female Combatants: A Case Study of the Gender Mainstreaming of DDR in Liberia." Master's thesis, Institute for Political Science, Universitetet i Oslo.

Ciment, James. 2013. *Another America: The Story of Liberia and the Former Slaves Who Ruled It.* New York: Hill and Wang.

Coalition to Stop the Use of Child Soldiers. 2008. *Returning Home: Children's Perspectives on Reintegration, A Case Study of Children Abducted by the Lord's Resistance Army in Teso, Eastern Uganda.* London: CSUCS.

Cohn, I., and G. S. Goodwin-Gill. 1994. *Child Soldiers: The Role of Children in Armed Conflict*. Oxford: Oxford University Press.

Cole, J., and D. L. Durham. 2007. *Generations and Globalization: Youth, Age, and Family in the New World Economy*. Bloomington: Indiana University Press.

Collier, P., and A. Hoeffler. 2004. "Greed and Grievance in Civil War." *Oxford Economic Papers* 56 (4): 563–595.

Collier, P., A. Hoeffler, and D. Rohner. 2006. *Beyond Greed and Grievance: Feasibility and Civil War*. Washington, DC: World Bank.

Cooper, E., and D. Pratten. 2015. "Ethnographies of Uncertainty in Africa: An Introduction." In *Ethnographies of Uncertainty in Africa*, edited by Elizabeth Cooper and David Pratten. Basingstoke: Palgrave Macmillan.

Coulter, C. 2009. *Bush Wives and Girl Soldiers: Women's Lives through War and Peace in Sierra Leone*. Ithaca: Cornell University Press.

Coulter, C., M. Persson, and M. Utas. 2010. *Young Female Fighters in African Wars: Conflict and Its Consequences*. Policy Dialogue No. 3. Uppsala: Nordic Africa Institute.

Coundouriotis, E. 2006. "The Dignity of the 'Unfitest': Victim's Stories in South Africa." *Human Rights Quarterly* 28 (4): 842–867.

Dahrendorf, R. 1981. *Life Chances: Approaches to Social and Political Theory*. Chicago: University of Chicago Press.

d'Azevedo, W. L. 1962. "Common Principles of Variant Kinship Structures among the Gola of Western Liberia." *American Anthropologist* 64 (3): 504–520.

———. 1969. "A Tribal Reaction to Nationalism (Part 1): Introduction." *Liberian Studies Journal* 1 (2): 1–22.

Denov, M. 2012. "Child Soldiers and Iconography: Portrayals and (Mis) Representations." *Children and Society* 26: 280–292.

Derluyn, I., E. Broekaert, G. Schuyten, and E. De Temmerman. 2004. "Post-Traumatic Stress in Former Ugandan Child Soldiers." *Lancet* 363: 861–863.

Di Nunzio, M. 2012. "'The Arada Have Been Eaten': Living through Marginality in Addis Ababa's Inner City." PhD diss., University of Oxford.

Durham, D. 2000. "Youth and the Social Imagination in Africa: Introduction to Parts 1 and 2." *Anthropological Quarterly* 73: 113–120.

Elbert, T., R. Weierstall, and M. Schauer. 2010. "Fascination Violence: On Mind and Brain of Man Hunters." *European Archives of Psychiatry and Clinical Neuroscience* 260 (1): 100–105.

Ellis, S. 2003. "Young Soldiers and the Significance of Initiation: Some Notes from Liberia." Paper presented at the Youth and the Politics of Generational Conflict in Africa conference, Afrika-Studiecentrum, Leiden.

Ember, C. R., and M. Ember. 2007. "A World Turned Upside Down: Social Ecological Approaches to Children in War." *Cross-Cultural Research* 41 (2): 96–122.

Ennew, J., and J. Swart-Kruger. 2003. "Introduction: Homes, Places and Spaces in the Construction of Street Children and Street Youth." *Children, Youth and Environments* 13 (1). Accessed May 27, 2011. http://colorado.edu/journals/cye.

Evans, K. 2007. "Concepts of Bounded Agency in Education, Work, and the Personal Lives of Young Adults." *International Journal of Psychology* 42 (2): 85–93.

Eyber, C., and A. Ager. 2004. "Researching Young People's Experiences of War: Participatory Methods and the Trauma Discourse in Angola." In *Children and Youth on the Frontlines: Ethnography, Armed Conflict and Displacement*, edited by J. Boyden and J. de Berry. Oxford: Berghahn Books.

Ferguson, J. 1999. *Expectations of Modernity: Myths and Meanings of Urban Life on the Zambian Copperbelt.* Berkeley: University of California Press.

———. 2013. "Declarations of Dependence: Labour, Personhood, and Welfare in Southern Africa." *Journal of the Royal Anthropological Institute*, n.s., 19: 223–242.

Fraenkel, M. 1964. *Tribe and Class in Monrovia.* Oxford: Oxford University Press.

Fulton, R. M. 1972. "The Political Structures and Functions of Poro in Kpelle Society." *American Anthropologist* 74 (5): 1218–1233.

Furlong, A. 2009. "Revisiting Transitional Metaphors: Reproducing Inequalities under the Conditions of Late Modernity." *Journal of Education and Work* 22 (5): 343–353.

———. 2013. *Youth Studies: An Introduction.* Abingdon: Routledge.

Furlong, A., and F. Cartmel. 2007. *Young People and Social Change: New Perspectives*. 2nd ed. Maidenhead: McGraw Hill, Open University Press.

Gates, S., and S. Reich. 2009. "Introduction." In *Child Soldiers in the Age of Fractured States*, edited by S. Gates and S. Reich. Pittsburgh: University of Pittsburgh Press.

Gear, S. 2002. "Now That the War Is Over: Ex-Combatants' Transition and the Question of Violence: A Literature Review." *Violence and Transition Series*. Johannesburg: Centre for the Study of Violence and Reconciliation. Online at http://www.csvr.org.za/wits/papers/papvt9.

Giddens, A. 1984. *The Constitution of a Society*. Cambridge: Polity.

Goffman, E. 1963. *Stigma: Notes on the Management of Spoiled Identity*. Englewood Cliffs, NJ: Prentice-Hall.

Goody, E. N. 1982. *Parenthood and Social Reproduction: Fostering and Occupational Roles in West Africa*. New York: Cambridge University Press.

Gunst, L. 1996. *Born Fi' Dead: A Journey through the Jamaican Posse Underworld*. New York: Henry Holt.

Guyer, J. I., and Samuel M. E. Belinga. 1995. "Wealth in People as Wealth in Knowledge: Accumulation and Composition in Equatorial Africa." *Journal of African History* 36 (1): 91–120.

Guyot, J. 2007. *Suffer the Children: The Psychosocial Rehabilitation of Child Soldiers as a Function of Peace-Building*. London: Coalition to Stop the Use of Child Soldiers.

Hamer, M. C. 2011. "Militarized Youth in Western Côte d'Ivoire: Who Are They? Why Did They Fight?" In *Understanding Collective Political Violence*, edited by Y. Guichaoua. Basingstoke: Palgrave Macmillan.

Harrell-Bond, B. 1975. *Modern Marriage in Sierra Leone: A Study of the Professional Group*. The Hague: Mouton.

Harris, D. 1999. "From 'Warlord' to 'Democratic' President: How Charles Taylor Won the 1997 Liberian Elections." *Journal of Modern African Studies* 37: 431–455.

Hart, J. 2008. "Displaced Children's Participation in Political Violence: Towards Greater Understanding of Mobilisation." *Conflict, Security, and Development* 8: 277–293.

Hecker, T., K. Hermenau, A. Maedl, T. Elbert, and M. Schauer. 2012. "Appetitive Aggression in Former Combatants—Derived from the Ongoing

Conflict in DR Congo." *International Journal of Law and Psychiatry* 35: 244–249.

Hirschi, T. 1969. *Causes of Delinquency*. Berkeley: University of California Press.

Hirschi, T., and M. R. Gottfredson. 1995. *Control Theory and the Life Course Perspective*. Stockholm: Brottsförebyggande rådet.

Hlophe, S. 1979. *Class, Ethnicity and Politics in Liberia: A Class Analysis of Power Struggles in the Tubman and Tolbert Administrations from 1944–1975*. Washington, DC: University Press of America.

Hoffman, D. 2011a. "Violence, Just in Time: War and Work in Contemporary West Africa." *Cultural Anthropology* 26 (1): 34–57.

———. 2011b. *The War Machines: Young Men and Violence in Sierra Leone and Liberia*. Durham, NC: Duke University Press.

Honwana, A. 2005. "Innocent and Guilty: Child-Soldiers as Interstitial and Tactical Agents." In *Makers and Breakers: Children and Youth in Postcolonial Africa*, edited by A. Honwana and D. Boeck. Oxford: James Currey.

Horton, S. A. P. 1994. *Liberia's Underdevelopment—In Spite of the Struggle: A Personal Analysis of the Underlying Reasons for Liberia's Underdevelopment*. Washington, DC: University Press of America.

Human Rights Watch. 1994. *Easy Prey: Child Soldiers in Liberia*. New York: Human Rights Watch.

———. 2004. "How to Fight, How to Kill: Child Soldiers in Liberia." February 2. New York: Human Rights Watch.

Iliffe, J. 2005. *Honour in African History*. Cambridge: Cambridge University Press.

International Labour Organization. 2013. *Global Employment Trends for Youth*. Geneva: ILO.

Isiugo-Abanihe, Uche C. 1985. "Child Fosterage in West Africa." *Population and Development Review* 11 (1): 53–73.

Jackson, M. 2006. *The Politics of Storytelling: Violence, Transgression, and Intersubjectivity*. Copenhagen: Museum Tusculanum, University of Copenhagen.

James, A., and A. Prout. 1990. *Constructing and Reconstructing Childhood: Contemporary Issues in the Sociological Study of Childhood*. London: Falmer Press.

Jarecki, E., director. 2012. *The House I Live In*. Documentary film. Al Jazeera Documentary Channel.

Jefferson, Thomas. 1811. "January 21 letter from Thomas Jefferson, Late President of the United States, to John Lynd." *African American Perspectives: Pamphlets from the Daniel A. P. Murray Collection, 1818–1907*. Library of Congress, Digital ID: lcrbmrp t1503; http://hdl.loc.gov/loc.rbc/lcrbmrp.t1503.

Jeffrey, C. 2010a. "Geographies of Children and Youth I: Eroding Maps of Life." *Progress in Human Geography* 34 (4): 496–505.

———. 2010b. "Timepass: Youth, Class, and Time among Unemployed Young Men in India." *American Ethnologist* 37 (3): 465–481.

———. 2012. "Geographies of Children and Youth II: Global Youth Agency." *Progress in Human Geography* 36 (2): 245–253.

Jennings, K. M. 2008. "Unclear Ends, Unclear Means: Reintegration in Postwar Societies: The Case of Liberia." *Global Governance* 14: 327–345.

Jensen, S. 2008. *Gangs, Politics and Dignity in Cape Town*. Oxford: James Currey.

Johnson Sirleaf, E. 2009. *This Child Will Be Great: Memoir of a Remarkable Life by Africa's First Woman President*. New York: Harper Collins.

Kanagaratnam, P., M. Raundalen, and A. E. Asbjørnsen. 2005. "Ideological Commitment and Post-traumatic Stress in Former Tamil Child Soldiers." *Scandinavian Journal of Psychology* 46: 511–520.

Kaplan, R. D. 1996. *The Ends of the Earth: A Journey at the Dawn of the 21st Century*. New York: Random House.

Khort, B. A., M. J. D. Jordans, E. Perera, R. Karki, S. Koirala, and N. Upadhaya. 2010. "Social Ecology of Child Soldiers: Child, Family, and Community Determinants of Mental Health, Psychosocial Well-Being, and Reintegration in Nepal." *Transcultural Psychiatry* 47 (5): 727–753.

Knight, M., and A. Özerdem. 2004. "Guns, Camps and Cash: Disarmament, Demobilization and Reinsertion of Former Combatants in Transitions from War to Peace." *Journal of Peace Research* 41 (4): 499–516.

Kopytoff, I., and S. Miers. 1977. "Africa's 'Slavery' as an Institution of Marginality." In *Slavery in Africa: Historical and Anthropological Perspectives*, edited by Suzanne Miers and Igor Kopytoff. Madison: University of Wisconsin Press.

Kuwert, P., C. Spitzer, J. Rosenthal, and H. J. Freyberger. 2008. "Trauma and Post-traumatic Stress Symptoms in Former German Child Soldiers of World War II." *International Psychogeriatrics* 20 (5): 1014–1018.

Lammers, E. 2006. *War, Refuge, and Self: Soldiers, Students and Artists in Kampala, Uganda*. Amsterdam: University of Amersterdam.

Langevang, T. 2008. "'We Are Managing!' Uncertain Paths to Respectable Adulthoods in Accra, Ghana." *Geoforum* 29: 2039–2047.

Lemarchand, R. 1989. "African Peasantries, Reciprocity and the Market: The Economy of Affection Reconsidered." *Cahiers d'Études Africaines* 29 (113): 33–67.

Lemasle, N. 2010. "Combatants' Disarmament: Do Command and Control Matter? A Comparison of Sierra Leone and Liberia." PhD diss., Northwestern University.

Levitt, J. I. 2005. *The Evolution of Deadly Conflict in Liberia: From 'Paternaltarianism' to State Collapse*. Durham, NC: Carolina Academic Press.

Liebenow, J. G. 1962. "Liberia." In *African One-Party States*, edited by G. M. Carter. Ithaca: Cornell University Press.

———. 1985. *Liberia: The Quest for Democracy*. Bloomington: Indiana University Press.

Lin, J. 2012. "Youth Bulge: A Demographic Dividend or a Demographic Bomb in Developing Countries?" In "Let's Talk about Development," a blog hosted by the World Bank, http://blogs.worldbank.org/developmenttalk/youth-bulge-a-demographic-dividend-or-a-demographic-bomb-in-developing-countries.

Lin, N. 1999. "Building a Network Theory of Social Capital." *Connections* 22 (1): 28–51.

Little, Kenneth. 1965. "The Political Function of the Poro. Part I." *Journal of the International African Institute* 35 (4): 349–365.

———. 1966. "The Political Function of the Poro. Part II." *Journal of the International African Institute* 36 (1): 62–72.

Lubkemann, S. C. 2008. *Culture in Chaos: An Anthropology of the Social Condition in War*. Chicago: University of Chicago Press.

Machel, G. 2001. *The Impact of War on Children*. London: Hurst and Company.

Mahar, H. C. 1990. "The Basic Theoretical Position." In *An Introduction to the Work of Pierre Bourdieu: The Practice of Theory*, edited by H. C. Mahar and C. Wilkes. London: Macmillan.

Mains, D. 2007. "Neoliberal Times: Progress, Boredom, and Shame among Young Men in Urban Ethiopia." *American Ethnologist* 34 (4): 659–673.

———. 2012. *Hope Is Cut: Youth, Unemployment, and the Future in Urban Ethiopia*. Philadelphia: Temple University Press.

———. 2013. "Friends with Money: Balancing Affection and Reciprocity among Young Men in Urban Ethiopia." *American Ethnologist* 40 (2): 335–346.

Malinowski, B. (1922) 1961. *Argonauts of the Western Pacific*. New York: E. P. Dutton.

Marks, Z. 2013. "The Internal Dynamics of Rebel Groups: Politics of Material Viability and Organizational Capacity, RUF Sierra Leone." PhD diss., Department of Politics and International Relations, University of Oxford.

Matthews, G. B. 1980. "The Formation of an Opposition Party in Liberia and the Political Reality: The Experience of the Progressive Peoples Party, Address of the Chairman of the Progressive Alliance of Liberia (PAL) Delivered at the University of Liberia on April 8, 1978." In *Dependence, Underdevelopment and Persistent Conflict—On the Political Economy of Liberia*, edited by E. Hinzen and R. Kappal. Bremen: Veroffentlichungen aus dem Ubersee-Museum Bremen.

Mauss, M. (1950) 1990. *The Gift: The Form and Reason of Exchange in Archaic Societies*. Abingdon: Routledge.

McDowell, L. 2003. *Redundant Masculinities? Employment Change and White Working Class Youth*. Oxford: Blackwell.

McKay, S. A., and M. Wessells. 2004. "Correspondence: Post-traumatic Stress in Former Ugandan Child Soldiers." *Lancet* 363: 1646.

McMullin, J. 2007. "Reintegration of Combatants: Were the Right Lessons Learned in Mozambique?" *International Peacekeeping* 11 (4): 625–643.

———. 2012. "Integration or Separation? The Stigmatisation of Ex-Combatants after War." *Review of International Studies* 39: 385–414.

———. 2013. *Ex-Combatants and the Post-Conflict State: Challenges of Reintegration*. Basingstoke: Palgrave Macmillan.

Medeiros, E. 2007. "Integrating Mental Health into Post-Conflict Rehabilitation: The Case of Sierra Leonean and Liberian 'Child Soldiers.'" *Journal of Health Psychology* 12 (3): 498–504.

Ministry of Youth and Sports. 2005. "National Youth Policy." Monrovia, Liberia.

Moran, M. H. 2006. *Liberia: The Violence of Democracy*. Philadelphia: University of Pennsylvania Press.

Muggah, R. 2009. *Security and Post-Conflict Reconstruction: Dealing with Fighters in the Aftermath of War*. Oxford: Routledge.

Murphy, W. P. 2003. "Military Patrimonialism and Child Soldier Clientalism in the Liberian and Sierra Leonean Civil Wars." *African Studies Review* 46: 62–87.

NCDDRR. 2006. "DDRRP Liberia Lessons Learnt and Summary." Retrieved October 21, 2008, from erc.undp.org/evaluationadmin/downloaddocument.html?docid=1283.

Newell, S. 2006. "Estranged Belongings: A Moral Economy of Theft in Abidjan, Côte d'Ivoire." *Anthropological Theory* 6 (2): 179–203.

———. 2012. *The Modernity Bluff: Crime, Consumption, and Citizenship in Côte d'Ivoire*. Chicago: University of Chicago Press.

Nordstrom, C. 1999. "Visible Wars and Invisible Girls, Shadow Industries, and the Politics of Not-Knowing." *International Feminist Journal of Politics* 1 (1): 14–33.

Norman, S., E. B. Elbogen, and P. P. Schnurr. 2014. "Research Findings on PTSD and Violence." U.S. Department of Veterans Affairs. http://www.ptsd.va.gov/professional/cooccurring/research_on_ptsd_and_violence.asp.

Osaghae, E. E. 1996. "Ethnicity, Class and the Struggle for State Power in Liberia." *Monograph Series 1/96*. Dakar: Council for the Development of Social Science Research in Africa (CODESRIA).

Outram, Q. 1997. "'It's Terminal Either Way': An Analysis of Armed Conflict in Liberia, 1989–1996." *Review of African Political Economy* 73: 355–377.

Özerdem, A. 2012. "A Re-conceptualisation of Ex-Combatant Reintegration: 'Social Reintegration' Approach." *Conflict, Security & Development* 12 (1): 51–73.

Persson, M. 2012. "Demobilized and Remobilized? Lingering Rebel Structures in Post-War Liberia." In *African Conflicts and Informal Power: Big Men and Networks*, edited by M. Utas. London: Zed Books.

Peters, K. 2007. "From Weapons to Wheels: Young Sierra Leonean Ex-Combatants Become Motorbike Taxi-Riders." *Journal of Peace, Conflict & Development* 10: 1–23.

———. 2011. *War and the Crisis of Youth in Sierra Leone*. Cambridge: Cambridge University Press

Podder, S. 2011. "Child Soldier Recruitment in the Liberian Civil Wars: Individual Motivations and Rebel Group Tactics." In *Child Soldiers: From Recruitment to Reintegration*, edited by A. Özerdem and S. Podder. Basingstoke: Palgrave Macmillan.

———. 2012. "From Recruitment to Reintegration: Communities and Ex-Combatants in Post-Conflict Liberia." *International Peacekeeping* 19 (2): 186–202.

Pugel, J. B. 2007. *What Fighters Say: A Survey of Ex-Combatants in Liberia, February-March 2006*. New York: United Nations Development Program.

Putnam, R. D. 1995. "Bowling Alone: America's Declining Social Capital." *Journal of Democracy* 6 (1): 65–78.

Reno, W. 1998. *Warlord Politics and African States*. Boulder, CO: Lynne Rienner.

Resnick, D., and J. Thurlow. 2015. *African Youth and the Persistence of Marginalization: Employment, Politics, and Prospects for Change*. Abingdon: Routledge.

Richards, P. 1995. "Rebellion in Liberia and Sierra Leone: A Crisis of Youth?" In *Conflict in Africa*, edited by O. Furley. London: Tauris Academic Studies.

———. 1996. *Fighting for the Rain Forest: War, Youth and Resources in Sierra Leone*. Oxford: James Currey.

———. 2006. "Young Men and Gender in War and Postwar Reconstruction: Some Comparative Findings from Liberia and Sierra Leone." In *The Other Half of Gender: Men's Issues in Development*, edited by I. Bannon and M. C. Correia. Washington, DC: World Bank.

Rinehart, R. 1985. "Historical Setting." In *Liberia: A Country Study*, edited by H. D. Nelson. Washington, DC: Foreign Area Studies, American University.

Rosen, D. 2007. "Child Soldiers, International Humanitarian Law, and the Globalization of Childhood." *American Anthropologist* 109 (2): 296–306.

Sahlins, M. 1963. "Poor Man, Rich Man, Big-Man, Chief: Political Types in Melanesia and Polynesia." *Comparative Studies in Society and History* 5: 285–303.

———. 1965. "On the Sociology of Primitive Exchange." In *The Relevance of Models for Social Anthropology*, edited by Max Cluckman and Fred Eggan. New York: Frederick A. Praeger.

Sawyer, A. 1992. *The Emergence of Autocracy in Liberia: Tragedy and Challenge*. San Fransisco: ICS Press.

Schafer, J. 2001. "Guerrillas and Violence in Mozambique: De-socialization or Re-socialization?" *African Affairs* 100: 215–237.

———. 2004. "The Use of Patriarchal Imagery in the Civil War in Mozambique and Its Implications for the Reintegration of Child Soldiers." In *Children and Youth on the Front Line: Ethnography, Armed Conflict and Displacement*, edited by J. Boyden and J. de Berry. Oxford: Berghahn Books.

———. 2007. *Soldiers at Peace: Veterans and Society after the Civil War in Mozambique*. New York: Palgrave Macmillan.

Schwab, G. 1947. *Tribes of the Liberian Hinterland*. Cambridge, MA: Peabody Museum.

Sewell, W. H. 1992. "A Theory of Structure: Duality, Agency, and Transformation." *Journal of American Sociology* 98: 1–29.

Shaw, R. 2000. "'Tok Af, Lef Af': A Political Economy of Temne Techniques of Secrecy and Self." In *African Philosophy as Cultural Inquiry*, edited by Ivan Karp and D. A. Masolo. Bloomington: Indiana University Press.

Shepler, S. A. 2005. "Conflicted Childhoods: Fighting over Child Soldiers in Sierra Leone." PhD diss., University of California, Berkeley.

———. 2014. *Childhood Deployed: Remaking Child Soldiers in Sierra Leone*. New York: New York University Press.

Shick, T. W. 1977. *Behold the Promised Land: A History of Afro-American Settler Society in Nineteenth-Century Liberia*. Baltimore: Johns Hopkins University Press.

Singer, P. W. 2006. *Children at War*. Berkeley: University of California Press.

———. 2010. "The Enablers of War: Causal Factors behind the Child Soldiers." In *Child Soldiers in an Age of Fractured States*, edited by S. Gates and S. Reich. Pittsburgh: University of Pittsburgh Press.

Sommers, M. 2003. *Urbanization, War, and Africa's Youth at Risk: Towards Understanding and Addressing Future Challenges.* Atlanta: CARE; Washington, DC: Creative Associates International.

Spear, J. 2002. "Disarmament and Demobilisation." In *The Implementation of Peace Agreements*, edited by S. J. Stedman, D. Rothchild, and E. M. Cousens. Boulder, CO: Lynne Rienner.

Spencer, P. 1965. *The Samburu: A Study of Gerontocracy in a Nomadic Tribe.* London: Routledge and Kegan Paul.

Stebbins, G. B. 1853. *Facts and Opinions Touching the Real Origin, Character, and Influence of the American Colonization Society: Views of Wilberforce, Clarkson, and Others, and the Opinions of the Free People of Color in the United States.* New York: Negro Universities Press.

Stewart, E. A., R. L. Simons, and R. D. Conger. 2002. "Assessing Neighborhood and Social Psychological Influences on Childhood Violence in an African-American Sample." *Criminology* 40 (4): 801–829.

Stewart, F. 2008. "Horizontal Inequalities and Conflict: An Introduction and Some Hypotheses." In *Horizontal Inequalities and Conflict: Understanding Group Violence in Multiethnic Societies*, edited by F. Stewart. New York: Palgrave Macmillan.

Summerfield, D. 1999. "A Critique of Seven Assumptions behind Psychological Trauma Programmes in War-Affected Areas." *Social Science & Medicine* 48: 1449–1462.

Sutherland, E. H. 1956. *On Analyzing Crime.* Chicago: University of Chicago Press.

UN. 2010. "Second Generation Disarmament, Demobilization and Reintegration (DDR) Practices in Peace Operations: A Contribution to the New Horizon Discussion on Challenges and Opportunities for UN Peacekeeping." New York: United Nations Department of Peacekeeping Operations.

———. 2013. "UN Projects Aim to Help Liberian Refugees Reintegrate into Their Homeland." March 11. New York: UN News Centre.

———. 2016a. "Disarmament, Demobilization and Reintegration." Accessed March 28, 2016. http://www.un.org/en/peacekeeping/issues/ddr.shtml, .

———. 2016b. "Root Causes of Child Recruitment." Office of the Special Representative of the Secretary-General for Children and Armed Conflict. Accessed March 28, 2016. https://childrenandarmedconflict.un.org/effects-of-conflict/root-causes-of-child-soldiering/.

UNDP. 2003–2004. "Liberia Disarmament, Demobilization and Reintegration Programme (DDRR) Activity Report." United Nations Administered Trust Fund Report.

———. 2011. "Practice Note: Demobilization, Disarmement, and Reintegration of Ex-Combatants." New York: UNDP.

UN Secretary-General. 2005. "Note to the General Assembly." May. A/C.5/59/31.

Urdal, H. 2004. *The Devil in the Demographics: The Effect of Youth Bulges on Domestic Armed Conflict 1950–2000*. Washington, DC: World Bank.

———. 2006. "A Clash of Generations? Youth Bulges and Political Violence." *International Studies Quarterly* 50: 607–629.

U.S. State Department. 2015. "Founding of Liberia, 1847." https://history.state.gov/milestones/1830–1860/liberia.

Utas, M. 2003. "Sweet Battlefields: Youth and the Liberian Civil War." Uppsala: Department of Cultiral Anthropology and Ethnology, Uppsala University.

———. 2005a. "Building a Future? The Reintegration and Remarginalisation of Youth in Liberia." In *No Peace, No War: An Anthropology of Contemporary Armed Conflicts*, edited by P. Richards. Oxford: James Currey.

———. 2005b. "Victimcy, Girlfriending, Soldiering: Tactic Agency in a Young Woman's Social Navigation of the Liberian War Zone." *Anthropological Quarterly* 78: 403–430.

———. 2008. "Abject Heroes: Marginalised Youth, Modernity and Violent Pathways of the Liberian Civil War." In *Years of Conflict: Adolescence, Political Violence and Displacement*, edited by J. Hart. Oxford: Berghahn Books.

———. 2012. "Introduction: Bigmanity and Network Governance in Africa Conflicts." In *African Conflicts and Informal Power: Big Men and Networks*, edited by M. Utas. New York: Zed Books.

van der Kraaij, F. P. M. 1983. *The Open Door Policy of Liberia: An Economic History of Modern Liberia*. Bremen: Im Selbstverlag des Museums.

Vermeij, L. 2011. "Socialization and Reintegration Challenges: A Case Study of the Lord's Resistance Army." In *Child Soldiers: From Recruitment to Reintegration*, edited by A. Özerdem and S. Podder. Basingstoke: Palgrave Macmillan.

Vigh, H. 2006a. *Navigating Terrains of War: Youth and Soldiering in Guinea-Bissau*. Oxford: Berghahn Books.

———. 2006b. "Social Death and Violent Life Chances." In *Navigating Youth, Generating Adulthood: Social Becoming in an African Context*, edited by C. Christiansen, M. Utas, and H. E. Vigh. Uppsala: Nordiska Afrikainstitutet.

———. 2009. "Motion Squared: A Second Look at the Concept of Social Navigation." *Anthropological Theory* 9 (4): 419–439

———. 2011. "Critical States and Cocaine Connections: Figuring the State of Decay in Bissau." Evans-Pritchard Lecture presented at All Souls College, Oxford, May 4.

Walker, G., J. Wood, C. Millar, and E. Allemano. 2009. *Liberia Youth Fragility Assessment*. Washington, DC: U.S. Agency for International Development.

Waugh, Colin M. 1978. *Economy and Society: An Outline of Interpretative Sociology*. Berkeley: University of California Press.

———. 2011. *Charles Taylor and Liberia: Ambition and Atrocity in Africa's Lone Star State*. New York: Zed Books.

Weber, M. (1904) 2004. "The 'Objectivity' of Knowledge in Social Science and Social Policy." In *The Essential Weber: A Reader*, edited by S. Whimster. London: Routledge.

Weierstall, R., R. Haer, L. Banholzer, and T. Elbert. 2013. "Becoming Cruel: Appetitive Aggression Released by Detrimental Socialization in Former Congolese Soldiers." *International Journal of Behavioral Development* 37 (6): 505–513.

Welmers, W. E. 1949. "Secret Medicines, Magic, and Rites of the Kpelle Tribe in Liberia." *Southwestern Journal of Anthropology* 5 (3): 208–243.

Wrubel, T. P. 1971. "Liberia: The Dynamics of Continuity." *Journal of Modern African Studies* 9: 189–204.

Yule, W. 2000. "From Pogroms to 'Ethnic Cleansing': Meeting the Needs of War-Affected Children." *Journal of Child Psychology and Psychiatry* 41 (6): 695–702.

Zack-Williams, T. B. 2001. "Child Soldiers in the Civil War in Sierra Leone." *Review of African Political Economy* 28 (87): 73–82.

Zeitlyn, D. 2008. "Life-History Writing and the Anthropological Silhouette." *Social Anthropology* 16 (2): 154–171.

Index

About the Author

ABBY HARDGROVE teaches at Kipp Central City Academy in New Orleans, Louisiana. Prior to making her home in the Big Easy, Abby worked as a program leader with Thinking Beyond Borders, an international experiential learning program for gap-year students. As a scholar, her work focuses on the life chances of young men in depleted socioeconomic circumstances. She has conducted research with young people in Great Britain and in Liberia through the School of Geography and the Environment and the Department of International Development at the University of Oxford. She believes that our greatest challenges and our deepest joys are to be found in one another.

Available Titles in the Rutgers Series in Childhood Studies

Race in the Schoolyard: Negotiating the Color Line in Classrooms and Communities, Amanda E. Lewis

At Play in Belfast: Children's Folklore and Identities in Northern Ireland, Donna M. Lanclos

In Sickness and in Play: Children Coping with Chronic Illness, Cindy Dell Clark

Rethinking Childhood, Peter B. Pufall and Richard P. Unsworth, editors

Armies of the Young: Child Soldiers in War and Terrorism, David M. Rosen

Imagined Orphans: Poor Families, Child Welfare, and Contested Citizenship in London, Lydia Murdoch

Vietnam's Children in a Changing World, Rachel Burr

Girls in Trouble with the Law, Laurie Schaffner

Growing Girls: The Natural Origins of Girls' Organizations in America, Susan A. Miller

Designing Modern Childhoods: History, Space, and the Material Culture of Children, Marta Gutman and Ning de Coninck-Smith, editors

Risky Lessons: Sex Education and Social Inequality, Jessica Fields

Inventing Modern Adolescence: The Children of Immigrants in Turn-of-the-Century America, Sarah E. Chinn

Pleasures and Perils: Girls' Sexuality in a Caribbean Consumer Culture, Debra Curtis

Children and Childhood in American Religions, Don S. Browning and Bonnie J. Miller-McLemore, editors

Translating Childhoods: Immigrant Youth, Language, and Culture, Marjorie Faulstich Orellana

Children and Childhood in World Religions, Don S. Browning and Marcia J. Bunge, editors

We Fight to Win: Inequality and the Politics of Youth Activism, Hava Rachel Gordon

Between Good and Ghetto: African American Girls and Inner-City Violence, Nikki Jones

Contesting Childhood: Autobiography, Trauma, and Memory, Kate Douglas

Girlhood: A Global History, Jennifer Helgren and Colleen Vasconcellos

The Child in Film: Tears, Fears, and Fairy Tales, Karen Lury

Raising Your Kids Right: Children's Literature and American Political Conservatism, Michelle Ann Abate

Rights and Wrongs of Children's Work, Michael Bourdillon, Deborah Levison, William Myers, and Ben White

Disrupted Childhoods: Children of Women in Prison, Jane A. Siegel

Their Time Has Come: Youth with Disabilities on the Cusp of Adulthood, Valerie Leiter

Learning the Hard Way: Masculinity, Place, and the Gender Gap in Education, Edward W. Morris

Learning Race, Learning Place: Shaping Racial Identities and Ideas in African American Childhoods, Erin N. Winkler

Ambivalent Encounters: Childhood, Tourism, and Social Change in Banaras, India, Jenny Huberman

Children of the Occupation: Japan's Untold Story, Walter Hamilton

Life on the Malecón: Children and Youth on the Streets of Santo Domingo, Jon M. Wolseth

Defining Student Success: The Role of School and Culture, Lisa M. Nunn

Kids in the Middle: How Children of Immigrants Negotiate Community Interactions for Their Families, Vikki S. Katz

Childhood in a Sri Lankan Village: Shaping Hierarchy and Desire, Bambi L. Chapin

Child Soldiers in the Western Imagination: From Patriots to Victims, David M. Rosen

Race among Friends: Exploring Race at a Suburban School, Marianne Modica

Trafficked Children and Youth in the United States: Reimagining Survivors, Elzbieta M. Gozdziak

Fantasies of Neglect: Imagining the Urban Child in American Film and Fiction, Pamela Robertson Wojcik

City Kids: Transforming Racial Baggage, Maria Kromidas

Why Afterschool Matters, Ingrid A. Nelson

Children as Caregivers: The Global Fight against Tuberculosis and HIV in Zambia, Jean Marie Hunleth

Life after Guns: Reciprocity and Respect among Young Men in Liberia, Abby Hardgrove

CPSIA information can be obtained
at www.ICGtesting.com
Printed in the USA
LVOW03s0139060417
529789LV00001B/1/P

9 780813 573472